Jehovah Rapha: God who heals

David Watson

Help for the journey…

GILEAD
B O O K S

First published in Great Britain, July 2010
9 8 7 6 5 4 3 2 1

Gilead Books Publishing
Corner Farm
West Knapton
Malton
North Yorkshire YO17 8JB

www.GileadBooks.com

Copyright © Anne Watson 2010

British Library Cataloguing-in-Publication Data:
A catalogue record for this book is available from the British Library.

ISBN-13: 978-0-9558099-6-5

The publisher makes every effort to ensure that the papers used in our books are made from trees that have been legally sourced from well-managed and credibly certified forests by using a printer awarded FSC & PEFC chain of custody certification.

Edited and compiled by Chris Hayes
Cover design by Dave Magill

ACKNOWLEDGEMENTS

Once again I am immensely grateful to Anne Watson, Douglas Greenfield and The Belfrey Trust for their encouragement and invaluable support for this project. Thank you to James Harris at Anchor Recordings for providing me with the original recordings, and to Elisabeth for efficiently producing a manuscript from the spoken word. Thanks also to David Burton for copy editing and Dave Magill for the cover photography and art work.

C J Hayes

OTHER TITLES IN THIS SERIES

LIVING FAITH: LESSONS FROM ABRAHAM

CONTENTS

CHAPTER ONE

HEALING: THE EVIDENCE OF GOD'S POWER

> *Then Peter said, 'Silver or gold I do not have, but what I do have I give you. In the name of Jesus Christ of Nazareth, walk.' Taking him by the right hand, he helped him up, and instantly the man's feet and ankles became strong.*
> (Acts 3:6,7)

This healing of a lame beggar was just one of the miraculous signs that were seen in the early days of the church. Indeed, Doctor Luke mentions that there were many of them:

> *Everyone was filled with awe at the many wonders and signs performed by the apostles.* (Luke 2:43)

Here, a miracle of healing prepared the ground for over two thousand people to become followers of Jesus. Because here was the evidence of God's power. Today, by and large, God's power is not so evident – at least not to the eyes of a non-believer. And therefore I want to look at the whole question of divine healing, with particular reference to this miracle of healing in Acts chapter 3.

The New Testament disciples were specifically commissioned by Christ to heal the sick. When he called the Twelve in Matthew chapter 12 he gave them authority over unclean spirits and to heal every disease and every infirmity. When he sent out the Seventy-Two in Luke chapter 10 he told them to go into every town and, wherever they went, to heal the sick. And when he gave his final word of authority and commission to all his disciples in Mark chapter 16, just before his ascension, he said this:

> *And these signs will accompany those who believe: In my name they will drive out demons; they will speak in new tongues; they will pick up snakes with their hands; and when they drink deadly poison, it will not hurt them at all; they will place their hands on sick people, and they will get well.* (Mark 16:17-18)

And it goes on to say,

> *Then the disciples went out and preached everywhere, and the Lord worked with them and confirmed his word by the signs that accompanied it.* (Mark 16:20)

And even if you happen to be someone who shares the view of some commentators who doubt that this is part of St Mark's gospel; it is still an historical fact that for nearly 800 years after the ascension of Christ, the Church continued this healing ministry. Until this vision of the Church, which was given by Christ, was snuffed out by idolatry and materialism. And by and large we still lack that vision. So that you get the story of a notice that appeared outside a church: 'healing service cancelled owing to sickness.' That's the kind of state we are in today!

However, before we go any further I want to look carefully at the place of healing today, because there is certainly a new and lively interest in the ministry of healing. Let us look at three questions which I am constantly being asked about healing.

Question 1: Doesn't God now heal through doctors?

Well, praise God, the answer is yes. Obviously he heals through doctors. But not always. The healings in the New Testament were first and foremost wonders and signs. They were both wonders to those who witnessed the healing and they were signs of the presence of the living God. Signs are the truth of the message of Christ.

> *Then the disciples went out and preached everywhere, and the Lord worked with them and confirmed his word by the signs that accompanied it'* (Mark 16:20)

I have often been very struck by those few words in Romans 15, where Paul explains how God had given him such a tremendous ministry wherever he went. He says that he won obedience from the Gentiles by word and deed, by the power of signs and wonders, by the power of the Holy Spirit. We know a great deal about the first of those, word and deed, but not so much about signs and wonders today.

God does heal through doctors and normal medical means - and ultimately all healing comes through him. I am not denying that. But when these healings take place, normally speaking, God is not the one who is glorified. People say, 'how wonderful Kate is; what a brilliant surgeon Mr Archer is.' But God is not glorified because Mr Archer, or Doctor Kay is praised. Therefore, in this materialistic age, I believe we need to see God at work in unmistakable power and that we should pray for this and expect it.

I remember a delightful man called Paul. He was a Nigerian Muslim and then became a very fine Christian. Muslims, by and large, are not easily converted, so I asked Paul one day. How were you converted? Were you impressed by the message of Christ? No, he said, he wasn't impressed at all. He had heard many different philosophies, many different religions and he wasn't particularly impressed with this one. How were you converted then? He said it was like this. 'I was at a meeting when I witnessed two miraculous healings. The first one was a deaf person who could hear instantly. I was quite impressed but not convinced because he might have been pretending his deafness. But then I actually saw someone who was lame or crippled with some deformity. And I saw their twisted leg heal just like that, straighten out and heal before my very eyes. And then I said, this is the living God. This is the message I must believe in.'

A missionary doctor friend of mine who was showing slides in our church after a service spoke about his work in Nepal. He said that all the conversions in Nepal that he knew about had come through healing and deliverances from satanic power or from a direct vision of the Lord, all signs confirming the message which was heard.

Brother Andrew,[1] who has done a lot of work in Vietnam, told me recently that about 80 or 90 per cent of the conversions in Vietnam come through healing, where God confirms in a miraculous and dramatic way the truth of the message of Jesus Christ.

Question 2: Miracles can't happen - surely they go against some scientific law?

Well, this is such a common objection that it's worth dealing with it very briefly. But we should ask - what is a scientific law?

---

[1] Christian missionary famous for smuggling bibles into communist countries at the height of the Cold War, author of God's Smuggler

It's simply a generalisation of what normally happens. So when Newton goes on dropping apples one after another and they all fall to the ground, he devises a law of gravity. Christians would go further and say that scientific laws are generalisations of ways in which God normally acts. But there is no higher law which says that God must act like that always. As the Psalmist rightly said,

> Our God is in heaven;
> he does whatever pleases him.
> (Psalm 115:3)

A doctor once operated on a cancer patient and declared that the situation was quite hopeless. A friend of his was a Christian minister and, with the doctor's full permission, the Christian minister had a little healing service, where the patient was anointed with oil and prayed for. Almost immediately he recovered completely. The minister asked the doctor, 'how do you explain it?' The doctor just shrugged his shoulders and said, 'Well that is beyond me, that is beyond me.' Fully recognising - as I believe many doctors do - that God's power can break into any situation even when medically speaking it is impossible. There are some things beyond normal healing means.

Question 3: Isn't the salvation of the soul far more important than the healing of the body?

Undoubtedly I would say that is true. Jesus himself said,

> 'Do not be afraid of those who kill the body but cannot kill the soul. Rather, be afraid of the One who can destroy both soul and body in hell.' (Matthew 10:28)

11

In other words, spiritual realities are certainly the most important thing. When a person is born again by the Spirit of God, that is the greatest miracle that could ever be. St Paul said,

> *'...if anyone is in Christ, the new creation has come.'*
> (2 Corinthians 5:17).

However, divine healing, when rightfully used, can be a most powerful force evangelistically. Of course, it should never become the central part of the Christian message. I think this is the first time I have preached a complete sermon on healing from this pulpit or any other pulpit. I hope it is not the central part of our message in this church. It certainly is not in my reckoning.

But surely healing does reveal the compassion and power of Jesus Christ and should lead on to something even greater. When this cripple, in Acts chapter 3, was dramatically healed, what did Peter say? Did he say, 'now bring in all your sick and we'll have a wonderful healing service'? He said nothing of the kind. Instead, in verse 19 of this passage Peter declares,

> *'Repent, then, and turn to God, so that your sins may be wiped out, that times of refreshing may come from the Lord.'* (Acts 3:19)

He was far more concerned with spiritual salvation - that people should find Jesus Christ, turn away from their sins and put their trust in Him. The wonderful healing was a demonstration that Christ was alive, that this was true, that people could know Him. God forbid that our interest should be primarily in divine healing. If so, we shall lose our vision of things which are far, far more important. And it's because the church today has largely turned to mere humanitarian interests, concerned mostly with physical and mental needs of people, that the church has lost much of its spiritual power in a world which is full of spiritual darkness and evil. The Archbishop of York said to a number of leaders recently: 'Of course we should be concerned with the body and mind, but the spiritual needs are above all the most important.'

Well, let's turn more specifically to this healing in Acts chapter 3. I want you to notice also the context of this healing. It came shortly before the outpouring of the Spirit on the day of Pentecost, and the essence of this outpouring was that it brought home to the disciples the reality of the risen, living Christ, even though he was no longer seen. And it brought home to them the love of Jesus. They were all filled with the Spirit. So they had a wonderful fellowship where they worked together and prayed together and witnessed together, and loved one another in Jesus. Their faith was at a very high level. Their vision in God was great. They encouraged one another to speak and do tremendous things boldly in the name of Jesus. Now if only that were the hallmark of every Christian fellowship today, instead of what happens so often - petty little irritations, resentments, criticisms, jealousies and so on. You see, whenever you have a fresh outpouring of the Spirit of God, wonderful things can happen.

I had a letter from the doctor in Nepal and he said, 'We have seen amazing things in the past few months, starting among the missionaries. Six have been filled with the Spirit, one completely liberated from real bondage and her whole life and outlook transformed in a way that everyone can see. In the leprosy hospital we have seen several people healed - two instantly, and another made dramatic progress in one month that would normally take four years'. God has poured out his

Spirit in a new way among the Christians, and at once things begin to happen.

When the Holy Spirit's power is at work not just in individuals but in the whole fellowship, then astounding things can happen. Where the atmosphere is not that of faith and love, then maybe nothing will happen. Do you remember how Jesus, in his own home church in Nazareth, said that he couldn't do many mighty works because of their lack of faith, in Matthew 13:58?

I think that is striking. Imagine if Jesus was here in the flesh and he was a regular member of this congregation. Just imagine the Son of God as a regular member here, and yet people in this congregation are not healed. That's what it was like in his home town because they didn't really believe. If this fellowship here is not full of faith and love, we will not see healings, we will not see many signs of God's power.

The context of healing is so important. Verse one describes the context of this healing, *'...Peter and John were going up to the temple at the time of prayer, at three in the afternoon.'* And back in verse 46 of the previous chapter, *'every day they continued to meet together in the temple courts.'* So we see that they were often praying.

And again it is in this context of prayer, day by day, several times a day apparently, that they saw – that we shall see - God's power at work, but there is a price to be paid. If only we really mean business with him, then he will mean business with us. Remember how the disciples, in Mark chapter 9, felt powerless that they couldn't help a boy possessed with a spirit? And they were puzzled because Jesus came along and at once the boy was healed. They asked, why couldn't we do it? Jesus answered, because this kind can only come out by prayer and fasting.

Notice also the timing of the healing,

Now a man who was lame from birth was being carried to the temple gate called Beautiful, where he was put every day to beg from those going into the temple courts.
(Acts 3:2)

We're also told two other interesting things about him. It's quite clear he was a very well known figure, because in verses 9 and 10 all the people saw him walking and praising God and recognised him as the one who sat for hours at the Beautiful Gate of the temple. And we're told later, in chapter 4 verse 22, that he was over 40 years old. So he had been at this particular gate, which was a very well-known gate which lots of people went through when going to the temple. There he sat, day after day, year after year, for a very long time. This means that Jesus had passed him many times, because he had often been in the temple preaching and teaching. So he had passed by this cripple on many occasions. Why didn't he stop and heal him? Didn't he care? Why did he leave it for Peter and John?

Part of the answer is that this was one of those vital times when it was necessary to demonstrate to the people that this was the gospel of Christ. In all divine healing, especially when it comes to a prayer for healing, the sufferer must submit themselves entirely to the sovereign will of God, and acknowledge that his way is perfect and that his timing is perfect. Whether or not we understand what he is doing, whether or not we understand why it can be that one person is healed at a service and at the same service another person is not healed. Whether we understand this or not, we need to say humbly, as Job did, *'Though he slay me, yet will I hope in him.'* (Job 13:15) and *'The Lord gave, and the Lord has taken away, may the name of the Lord be praised.'* (Job 1:21b).

15

Whatever happens, I will praise his name. And although he gives us many promises of healing, and surely wants us to trust his promises and his word, I don't believe we can ever presume to command him to heal now, at this moment, unless he has made it clear that this is his will, and has given us specific gifts of faith for that occasion and for that purpose.

Now this is so important to understand – that you must submit your whole being to the sovereign will of God, that he knows what he is doing, that he understands what he is doing, whether we understand or not.

Briefly then, the particular healing itself. Perhaps the outstanding feature when I read this passage again was that the cripple wasn't full of faith himself at all. Indeed, he wasn't even asking for healing. As we see in verses 3 to 5,

> 'When he saw Peter and John about to enter, he asked them for money. Peter looked straight at him, as did John. Then Peter said, "Look at us!" So the man gave them his attention, expecting to get something from them.'

But certainly not healing, just money. Faith is necessary in divine healing, there is no doubt about that at all. Yet Peter goes on to say,

> 'By faith in the name of Jesus, this man whom you see and know was made strong. It is Jesus' name and the faith that comes through him that has completely healed him, as you can all see.' (Acts 3:16)

Faith is important. But the challenge of faith should not rest on the sick person alone or sometimes at all. Many sick people, when they are not healed after prayer, get very depressed. 'I haven't got enough faith. If only I had more faith.' And they feel very sad, very guilty that they've been inadequate in their faith in the Lord, and they get terribly in bondage about this.

Now that's wrong. I know personally that it's very, very difficult to be full of faith when you are ill. Most of us know that. The battle of faith happens very largely through the praying fellowship of believing Christians. It is a whole atmosphere of faith and love, the whole fellowship that counts. And even then, before there can be healing, there must normally be a specific gift of faith from God for that person, for that moment.

You can see all of this at work in this passage. You can see the authority of Peter and John. As Peter says in verse 6, *'Silver or gold I do not have, but what I do have I give you. In the name of Jesus Christ of Nazareth, walk!'* And immediately he stretched out his hands because he meant business, and lifted the man up - and he walked.

And why hadn't Peter and John done this before? They had no doubt passed by the man on many occasions. The answer is partly that after Pentecost their whole faith had risen, but also that God gave them a specific gift of faith for that moment. They knew God was going to act. Otherwise to say that would have been sheer presumption.

Finally, let's look at some of the wonderful results from this healing. First and foremost, Christ himself was glorified. In verse 12, when all the people rushed round Peter and John, simply amazed by what had happened, they say, *'People of Israel, why does this surprise you? Why do you stare at us as if by our own power or godliness we had made this man walk?'*

We can't do it; it's Jesus who does it. Jesus is glorified and this is always a supreme test for any so-called faith healer. I want to speak carefully, and I hope wisely, on this point. There are many faith healers today, and not all of them are from God, not by a long way. Most of the faith healers that I have read booklets from will talk about God and about the Holy Spirit. The real question is, where is Christ in their whole ministry and in their writings? Is Christ at the centre? Is he the one that is glorified? And if he is mentioned in some measure, is it in accordance with the teaching of Scripture? Is the cross central? Is there teaching about sin and forgiveness? Is the gospel there, or is it simply some kind of vague teaching which is nothing really to do with the gospel of Christ at all?

If not, then we should be very, very, wary indeed. Jesus warned us there would be those signs and wonders which would deceive even the very elect, those signs and wonders coming ultimately from Satan himself. And if you're seeking healing and you have some rather doubtful literature, maybe sent to you because you wrote off to some person meaning the very best, and you can't really see that Christ is central in that literature, then I would urge you to destroy it, as a serious sign that you want Christ's glory alone in whatever may happen to you.

As a sequel to the healing in this passage, not only were two thousand converted, but also the first wave of persecution began. And it came from religious people. The devil doesn't like it when God's power is manifested, there is always a price to pay if we really want God at work.

I believe God is asking each one of us, and certainly asking me, where is there a man or a woman who is going to take this seriously? I believe he's looking for someone who is going to be a worker together with him. He's looking for someone, indeed for a group of people, who are really going to pray and call upon his name, because he's got to see if he can trust my power with us. God doesn't throw his greatest gift at anyone. We need to be very humble about it. But may God grant that we will not miss his greatest purposes for our lives.

Let us pray.

Heavenly Father, we praise you that you have given us a Saviour who comes to save us entirely and cares for every part of our lives, who cares about our pain and sicknesses, our depressions and worries. We thank you that we can trust him and find him true in our own heart, even through the midst of suffering. We thank you for all that we can learn about you when we are going through times of darkness.

But Lord, we long that Christ will be manifestly glorified in our midst, that people should be able to see that you are the Living God, that people should know that this truth about Jesus is the truth, that people should tremble before him because they realise that he is on the throne of the universe. And all that we say about him and believe about him is absolutely true.

Lord, we believe that we are in the midst of a world that is unbelieving. And we ask for the glory of his name alone, that you will pour out your Spirit afresh upon us. Give us a new love for Jesus, a new faith to believe that with the Lord nothing is impossible. Guide us in our thinking about this great and difficult subject, Lord. But help us at all times wholly to trust Jesus. We ask this for the glory of his name.

Amen.

CHAPTER TWO

GROUNDS FOR HEALING

Let's be quiet in God's presence for a moment as we worship him in our hearts and praise him for his everlasting love.

A prayer:

Loving heavenly Father, we bless you that you are a God of love. God is love, your word says. We thank you that you so loved us that you gave your only begotten son, so that as we believe in him we shall not perish but have everlasting life. We thank you that your love is steadfast and surrounds us day by day, and we thank you for everything we have known of your love this very day.

We thank you that your mercies are new every morning. We thank you for the assurance of forgiveness through the blood of Jesus. We thank you for your love which says 'I will never leave you nor forsake you'. We thank you for your love, which says 'my grace is sufficient for you'. We thank you for your love, shown in all those great and precious promises in your word. We thank you for your faithfulness. We thank you that you look upon us as people with many different needs but each one individually loved by yourself. We bless you, Lord, for this is far too great for us to understand but we know that as the heavens are high above the earth, so great is your mercy and steadfast love towards those who fear you. We bless you for this, Heavenly Father, and we pray that, because you know our needs, you will open our eyes and above all give us the faith to trust you in your love and to rest in that everlasting love. So guide us as we look at this tremendously important subject, which affects us all. Help us to believe you and to trust you and above all to know that you love us. We ask this for Jesus Christ's sake.

Amen.

I hope you'll forgive me if I have a word of personal testimony right from the start, because I believe that the Lord has allowed something to happen in the last few days which is relevant to today's this subject - the grounds for healing. On Sunday night I had a touch of flu and felt fairly miserable by the end of the service. On Monday I felt a little bit better and we went out and did some shopping, but I felt fairly grim on Monday afternoon, then went to bed quite early that evening. On Tuesday I had a temperature of 39ºC and felt very rough indeed, for which I received some prayer that morning. I will refer to this later on because I think it is quite interesting to look at what we were praying for and what we were expecting to happen.

But in fact nothing happened. So I had a pretty miserable day just sleeping and lying there doing nothing very much. As my temperature was fluctuating but still over 39ºC by the afternoon we felt it right to ask the doctor to come because of previous chest complaints and concern that it might start up bronchitis trouble I've had over the last year. Well, the doctor came and prescribed one or two things. The next day my temperature fluctuated between 37ºC and 39ºC and that evening I thought, 'I really am rather childish to talk about grounds for healing, when here I am lying in bed feeling quite ill'.

So, as I was lying there feeling convicted about this, I was reading again some of the grounds for healing that we're going to look at now. And as I read them, feeling not at all well, the Lord said quite clearly, 'if this is true, why don't you act on it?' I was really convicted about these biblical grounds for healing. So last night I just got out of bed and said 'Lord, here I am trying to say to people that healing is to be found in your name, and here I am just lying in bed doing nothing about it. Forgive me for all this, and Lord I claim your healing now.' I thanked and praised the Lord, got up and went downstairs. The fever left me completely. I had something to eat and a very good night's sleep.

As I look at the grounds for healing I shall illustrate them from this recent experience - for which I really praise God. I have nine grounds for healing and then a few questions.

1. God's changeless character

I, the Lord, do not change. (Malachi 3:6)

Jesus Christ is the same yesterday and today and forever. (Hebrews 13:8)

God never changes - he has a changeless character - and in the Old Testament he revealed himself in what are called the seven redemptive names of God, seven names which give seven aspects of his character:

Jehovah Shammah: 'the Lord is present' (Ezekiel 48:35)
Jehovah Shalom: 'the Lord our peace,' (Judges 6:24)
Jehovah Ra-ah: 'the Lord my shepherd' (Psalm 23)
Jehovah Jireh: 'the Lord will provide' (Genesis 22:13,14)

Jehovah Nissi: 'the Lord our banner' (Exodus 17:8-15)
Jehovah Tsidkenu: 'the Lord our righteousness' (Jeremiah 23:6)
Jehovah Rapha: 'the Lord our healer' (Exodus 15:26)

All of these are eternally true. And interestingly, all of these are only true in your experience and in my experience through the atonement – through the death of Jesus Christ. We are only brought to God's presence as Jehovah Shamma in the first place through the blood of Jesus. But once God is with us, once we're with God, then he says, *'I will never leave you nor forsake you.'* (Hebrews 13:5) The Lord is here, **the Lord is present**.

The Lord our Peace. God made peace by the blood of his cross, by the blood of Jesus. Once we've come to Jesus, and come to know peace with God, we can experience *'the peace of God which transcends all understanding'.* (Philippians 4:7)

The Lord is my Shepherd. Remember Jesus said that as a shepherd he would lay down his life for the sheep. (John 10:15)

The Lord will Provide. The context of this is as Abraham is about to offer up his son Isaac as a sacrifice. It's the knowledge that the Lord will provide an offering for Abraham to give instead of his son. And Jesus was the offering that God ultimately provided. Again this refers to the idea of the cross. And the cross is a guarantee that the Lord will provide everything - all - because God, *'...who did not spare his own Son, but gave him up for us all, how will he not also, along with him, graciously give us all things?'* (Romans 8:32)

The Lord is our banner, (or the Lord is our victor, the Lord is our conqueror). Now where did he conquer Satan? He conquered him on the cross so that you and I can be *'more than conquerors through him that loved us'.* (Romans 8:37)

The Lord is our righteousness. Remember how Paul said, *'God made him who had no sin to be sin for us, so that in him we* *might become the righteousness of God'*? (2 Corinthians 5:21) That is we are right with God, by faith in Jesus.

The Lord is all these things, and bears all these names. They are eternal, and he is all these things to us now. We know that. No Christian should doubt that for one moment. But the seventh name, which is also eternal, which also applies today is this: **The Lord our healer**. Jehovah Rapha. And again, it seems that the blessings of God's healing are made possible through the atonement, through the death of Jesus Christ.

It's interesting that this particular revelation of God's name comes just after the crossing of the Red Sea, which is a great picture of our own salvation. Israel were brought out of slavery in Egypt and immediately the Lord reveals himself:

> *Then Moses led Israel from the Red Sea and they went into the Desert of Shur. For three days they travelled in the desert without finding water. When they came to Marah, they could not drink its water because it was bitter. (That is why the place is called Marah). So the people grumbled against Moses, saying, 'What are we to drink?'*
> *Then Moses cried out to the Lord, and the Lord showed him a piece of wood. He threw it into the water, and the water became sweet.*
>
> *There the Lord issued a ruling and instruction for them and put them to the test. He said, 'If you listen carefully to the Lord your God and do what is right in his eyes, if you pay attention to his commands and keep all his decrees, I will not bring on you any of the diseases I brought on the Egyptians, for I am the Lord, who heals you.* (Exodus 15:22-26)

This is one of the great moments of biblical history, when God revealed himself right after that time of salvation. *'I am the Lord who heals you.'* Now following that, I think everyone agrees that the blessings of the Old Testament are only a shadow of the blessings of the New Testament. The New Testament is far richer. The Old Testament people were in slavery to endless rites and sacrifices. We now look back to the once-for-all, glorious sacrifice of Jesus on the cross (Hebrews 10:10). And if all the blessings of the New Testament are far richer and more wonderful, who could possibly say that God has removed one of the vital blessings of the Old Testament, that in some measure he is no longer what he was, in some measure he has withdrawn something which obviously matters tremendously in the lives of people in their ordinary everyday lives?

It's inconceivable that God has cut away one-seventh of his character and has said 'I am no longer this - I was this but I am not now'. Surely today he is still what he revealed himself to be - and clearly here his healing is not just spiritual. Clearly he is still the Lord our healer. This is the first ground that I think we can stand firmly on. The Lord is our healer; he is concerned about our bodies and minds, as well as our souls.

2. Christ's finished work at Calvary

I would like to look at two passages here,

> *When Jesus came into Peter's house, he saw Peter's mother-in-law lying in bed with a fever. He touched her hand and the fever left her, and she got up and began to wait on him. When evening came, many who were demon-possessed were brought to him, and he drove out the spirits with a word and healed all the sick.* (Matthew 8:14-16)

And then notice what it goes on to say in verse 17:

> *This was to fulfil what was spoken through the prophet Isaiah: "He took up our* (not just sins, but he took our) *infirmities and bore our diseases."*

You will probably recognise this as a reference to Isaiah 53:4, as a great prophecy in the Old Testament referring to the atonement of the cross of Jesus Christ. There he bore not only our sins and iniquities but - according to God's own commentary - he took our infirmities and bore our diseases. It's worthwhile to have a look at another two verses from Isaiah here:

> *Surely he took up our pain and bore our suffering, yet we considered him punished by God, stricken by him, and afflicted. But he was pierced for our transgressions, he was crushed for our iniquities; the punishment that brought us peace was on him, and by his wounds we are healed.* (Isaiah 53:4,5)

Jesus died on the cross for our sicknesses, for our pains, for our transgressions, for our iniquities, for our sins, for our peace and for our healing. He died for all these things, not just for our sins, but also according to scripture itself, for our sicknesses and our pains as well.

Later, you will remember that Paul says Christ has redeemed us from the curse of the law by becoming a curse for us (Galatians 3:13). Part of the curse of the law was physical disease, and he has taken away that curse through his death upon the cross. I believe that there is tremendous healing power in the cross of Jesus Christ. If there is to be healing at all in the church, in the ordinary course of church services and worship, I think that the most likely time for it to happen is in a communion service, where people are concentrating on the cross of Jesus Christ, concentrating upon the blood of Jesus.

A personal illustration of this is when Anne and I were at a conference on revival and there was a communion service toward the end of the conference. For a year Anne had trouble with some sort of skin infection on her finger, for which she had tried practically every sort of ointment. At this conference she wasn't thinking of asking for prayer for the healing of this irritation. But she simply went to the communion service like everybody else and when she came out from the service, she realised that the infection had completely gone. Anne wasn't concentrating, her illness, but simply on the blood of Jesus - and that brought about the healing needed.

One book which I have found very helpful in the question of healing is called 'Christ the Healer', by F.F. Bosworth, who describes one particular case:

> 'I will now cite one out of many hundreds of cases of sickness and affliction that have been healed while the sufferers listened to the preaching on the subject of healing in the atonement...When she was just a child of 8 years, Mrs Clara Rupert of Lima, Ohio, had such a severe case of whooping cough that she ruptured the muscles of one eye. This left it entirely blind and so dead during all the years that followed that she could rub her finger on the bare eyeball without pain. She said that on windy days, when particles were blown into the eye, it caused her no suffering.
>
> She was listening to a sermon on the atonement during our revival in Lima, Ohio. She said in her heart: "if that is

true, and it is because the bible says so, then I am just as sure of receiving sight in my blind eye tonight when I go to the altar as I was sure of salvation when I went to that Methodist altar...and was saved." With this logical reasoning, she came to the altar, and while we were praying with others, she asked God to heal her. Before we had a chance to anoint her, she was on her feet weeping. She walked back and threw her arms around her father's neck. The audience wondered why she left the altar without being anointed. Her father said: "What is the matter, daughter?" She replied, "My eye." He said: "Why, is it paining you?" She said: "No I can see perfectly!"' [2]

Here is someone who was just concentrating on the atonement and she was healed. There is healing in the cross of Christ.

3. Christ's own earthly ministry

We could spend a long time looking at this, but we will take just a few verses from Matthew's gospel, to see that when we are praying for healing we are not doing a kind of vague, shadowy thing but something absolutely firm - rock-like. That's what hit me last night when I was lying very ill with flu. Suddenly I realised how solid the ground for healing was; so I got out of bed and stood on it.

Jesus went throughout Galilee, teaching in their synagogues, proclaiming the good news of the kingdom, and healing every disease and sickness among the people. News about him spread all over Syria, and people brought

[2] Bosworth, F.F. (2008) Christ the Healer, Revised edition, Chosen Books (A division of Baker Publishing Group), p45f

to him all who were ill with various diseases, those suffering severe pain, the demon-possessed, those having seizures, and the paralyzed; and he healed them.
(Matthew 4:23,24)

Aware of this, Jesus withdrew from that place. A large crowd followed him, and he healed all who were ill.
(Matthew 12:15)

And when the men of that place recognized Jesus, they sent word to all the surrounding country. People brought all their sick to him and begged him to let the sick just touch the edge of his cloak, and all who touched him were healed.
(Matthew 14:35,36)

Now, we could go on turning over page after page in the gospels and we would find similar examples. Is there ever the faintest suggestion anywhere that Christ ever said to anyone, 'well I'm sorry, but you must put up with it?' And 'don't worry, I'm sure God will help you and give you peace.' No. He never, ever gave that impression. His earthly ministry was concrete - he healed all who were brought to him or who touched him with faith.

4. Christ's promise to his disciples

Very truly I tell you, all who have faith in me will do the works I have been doing, and they will do even greater things than these, because I am going to the Father. And I will do whatever you ask in my name, so that the Father may be glorified in the Son. You may ask me for anything in my name, and I will do it. (John 14:12-14)

Jesus is not just talking to the apostles here, people who may be very specially equipped with some power from above. No, he says *'all who have faith in me will do the works I have been doing.'* That refers to every single one of us. If we believe in him, he promises that we shall be able to do the kind of things that he did. And of course the early disciples experienced this, and you find it was the case right the way through the Acts of the Apostles. In Acts chapter 28, thirty years or so after Christ's ascension into heaven, you still find exactly the same pattern. There was no diminishing of this power once the church was on its feet.

Incidentally, when was there a generation when the church did *not* need to be put on its feet? If people believe these gifts of the spirit were simply to get the church established, surely we can expect there to be healings today because we still need the church to be established in this country as well as everywhere else. But it wasn't of course, just for that. It's a constant pattern. In Acts 28: verses eight and nine on the island of Malta, Paul was shown hospitality by Publius, the chief official:

> *His father was sick in bed, suffering from fever and dysentery. Paul went in to see him and, after prayer, placed his hands on him and healed him. When this had happened, the rest of the sick on the island came and were cured.*

You can't help but see that in Acts, healing was a tremendous evangelistic force. It wasn't that these people had now got sidetracked and they were just involved with healings and no longer concerned with evangelism. That can be a danger; it *can* happen but there is no reason why it *should*: healing properly leads to God being glorified.

31

Great crowds came to him, bringing the lame, the blind, the crippled, the mute and many others, and laid them at his feet; and he healed them. The people were amazed when they saw the mute speaking, the crippled made well, the lame walking and the blind seeing. And they praised the God of Israel. (Matthew 15:30-31)

Again, to quote F.F. Bosworth,[3]

'You'll notice that in the scriptures,[4] as the result of miracles of healing, Jesus' fame was spread broadly, and they came to him from every quarter, and they followed him on foot out of the cities, and great multitudes came to him, everywhere. It is the same today. As the command to make his deeds and his compassion known among the people is obeyed and his compassion is published, things begin to happen. As soon as it is heard in any city that Jesus is there, actually healing the sick, people come from every quarter. I have never seen anything that will break down barriers and bring the people from every quarter as much as the manifestation of the Lord's compassion in healing the sick. We found in our revivals that as soon as the public find out what Jesus is doing they come from every quarter...Multitudes hear the gospel and give their lives to God. They would never even attend the meetings if there were no healing miracles to reveal his compassion.'

And he says that,

---

[3] Op. cit. Bosworth, F. F (2008) p81f
[4] See also, Mark 5:19-20; Mark 1:40-45; Matthew 14:13-14; Matthew 20:29-34

'We preached for thirteen years before the Lord led us to preach this part of the gospel in a bolder and more public way...we have seen more happy conversions in a single week than we ever saw in a whole year of evangelistic work before.'

When there are special times of revival, people will crowd just to hear the simple, straightforward gospel being preached. But generally today, people do not do that. See how difficult it is to get people to come along to church services. People just aren't interested. But if they saw the Lord's compassion in this sort of way, people would come.

5. God's instructions and promise to any Christian who is sick

Is anyone among you sick? Let them call the elders of the church to pray over them and anoint them with oil in the name of the Lord. And the prayer offered in faith will make them well; the Lord will raise them up. If they have sinned, they will be forgiven. Therefore confess your sins to each other and pray for each other so that you may be healed. The prayer of a righteous person is powerful and effective. (James 5:14-16)

Just notice how this prayer wouldn't be like the prayers we are tempted to pray, 'Lord, if it is your will, may this happen...' James goes on to illustrate using Elijah.

Elijah was a human being, even as we are. He prayed earnestly that it would not rain, and it did not rain on the land for three and a half years. Again he prayed, and the

> *heavens gave rain, and the earth produced its crops.* (James
> 5:17-18)

You see, Elijah was a man like us and he prayed fervently – and
not 'if it be God's will'. He prayed fervently that it might not
rain, and for three years and six months it did not rain on the
earth. He really prayed – boldly, and for something specific. His
prayer was answered. The whole context of this is that we are
to pray very emphatically, knowing that it is God's will in this
situation.

But of course we need to say that there is a condition that has
to be fulfilled.

> *'Therefore confess your sins to each other and pray for*
> *each other so that you may be healed.'* (James 5:16)

There is often a need for some heart-searching, for some
confession, both to God and to one another, before we can
expect God to heal. Sickness is sometimes chastening for sin.
And if that is so, there cannot be healing until there is
repentance. But let me clarify this important point: sickness is
not always chastening. Sometimes it is just a direct attack of
Satan. Or it may just be allowed by God, as in the case of Job. His
sickness was a direct attack of Satan but allowed by God for a
period of time. The purpose of that is to lead you into a deeper
trust in the Lord before there is deliverance. We don't fully
understand the reasons why, and Job couldn't understand. It
must have gone on for a long time, but he came to a deeper trust
in God through this experience. But it wasn't chastening in his
case, nor is it in many other people's experience. But it is
important in the first instance that there should be some heart-
searching and confession.

If someone had asked me when I went to bed on Monday evening whether I thought my illness was chastening, I would probably have said, 'no, I don't think so' because I couldn't think of anything I felt I was being disobedient about. But on Tuesday morning when some people came to pray for me, I felt that God was really challenging me on a number of different points, some of which affect the fellowship as well as me. I felt that God was saying our worship was not what it might be; that it was superficial; and where was the prayer and praise? I accepted this and said, 'yes, Lord, I believe that this is one of the things you are trying to tell me, I need to be chastened along these lines': and there had to be repentance before we could go any further.

6. Our bodies are the dwelling place of the Holy Spirit

And if the Spirit of him who raised Jesus from the dead is living in you, he who raised Christ from the dead will also give life to your mortal bodies because of his Spirit who lives in you. (Romans 8:11)

We shall only see the perfect fulfilment of Christ's work in heaven. However, if you are a true Christian, at work in your body right now is none less than the mighty spirit of God who raised Jesus from the dead. Are we implying that the same mighty spirit of God who raised Jesus from the dead is unable to deal with the sicknesses and problems in our own lives? Of course not. Of course he can do it, and of course if our bodies are to be the temple of the Holy Spirit, surely he wants that temple to be as perfect as it can be.

7. Christ came to destroy the works of the devil

The reason the Son of God appeared was to destroy the devil's work. (1 John 3:8)

All sickness is ultimately due to sin, or we could say that sickness is ultimately due to Satan; Satan causing us to fall into sin. Therefore, if Christ came to destroy the works of the devil, surely he has come to destroy this particular work, the work of sickness and disease in the world. And again, isn't Christ concerned *today* about those who are oppressed by the devil in these different ways? Of course he is. He wants to destroy Satan's work in your body and in my body as well as in our souls.

8. Christ came for the whole person

This is an understanding of what the word 'save' means. You see, the very word 'save' which is used in the New Testament really means 'to make whole', 'to make sound', 'to heal'. It is as often used of physical healing as it is of spiritual salvation. It's the same word. God doesn't see us as little compartments of spirit, mind and body, and he certainly didn't come to save just one compartment. He sees us as one whole person. He comes to save the whole. And he is concerned with our bodies, minds, and spirits. Most important of all is our spiritual salvation because we will eventually have to leave these bodies behind one day, but he is concerned nevertheless with the whole person.

9. Jesus's love and compassion

I felt rebuked last night because I was thinking of Jesus as some sort of impersonal being that had power to heal, and was thinking as if I could somehow plug into that power for healing to happen. Then I realised, here is a living person who actually loves me. And it's the same for all the people that he met when he was here on this earth. When he saw a person's need he had compassion and did something for that person.

I love the hymn, 'Loved with everlasting love'[5] because you can so easily forget about the love of the Lord. You feel that he is there with a big stick behind you, driving you on, telling you that you must do this and you must do that. We forget that he loves us. He is concerned.

Sometimes we make the mistake of thinking that God is able to do heal, but not at all sure that he is willing to do it. Well, I believe that he longs to help us in his compassion, far, far more than we could ever imagine or ever realise. There's a lovely verse in Psalm 145,

> *The Lord is gracious and compassionate; slow to anger and rich in love. The Lord is good to all; he has compassion on all he has made.*
> (Psalm 145:8-9)

---

[5] Loved with everlasting love, led by grace that love to know;
Gracious Spirit from above, Thou hast taught me it is so!
O this full and perfect peace! O this transport all divine!
In a love which cannot cease, I am His, and He is mine.
(Words: George W. Robinson, 1876)

So if you have a problem at this moment, or a friend of yours has a problem, the Lord has compassion on you or on your friend. He really has.

Would you prefer me to say to you, 'I know that you would help me if you could' or 'I know that you can help me but I don't know if you are willing to'? Do you see the difference there? In the first instance, I show belief in your integrity that you would help me if you could. In the second I know that you can help me but I'm not at all sure if you are willing – which I think is a far more grieving thing to say. Yet this is roughly what we are saying to the Lord: I know you can help me but I am not sure if you are willing. I believe we need to trust him that he is able and willing *'to do immeasurably more than all we ask or imagine'* (Ephesians 3:20).

It is interesting that in one of the passages where Jesus shows his compassion to those who are sick and needy, wandering around like sheep having no shepherd, what he says is, *'Ask the Lord of the harvest, therefore, to send out workers into his harvest field'* (Matthew 9:38). In other words, you and I should go out to share the compassion of Jesus, to help people in all their needs, knowing that he, with us, can make a difference.

Finally, a few questions:

How can I receive healing?

Providing the conditions that I mentioned are fulfilled, the answer is, by faith. Though it's very important to understand what faith really means. Faith, you see, means believing God's word, claiming it to be true, and then acting as though it were already true.

Again, if I can give my testimony over these last few days, when I was prayed for on Tuesday morning I was lying there with a temperature. Friends prayed for me, they laid hands upon me, they prayed for healing, and I said, 'thank you, Lord', and just laid there waiting for something to happen. I still felt pretty wretched, so I thought to myself, 'well, it will come in God's good time.' I went back to sleep and went on being miserable for a couple more days. Now, last night when I felt rebuked, I realised that that wasn't faith at all, because when I had prayed for healing I was waiting for something to happen before I believed that God had really answered the prayer.

But the right way round is what God helped me to do last night, which was to pray, to claim, to believe, to thank God, and then get up and go downstairs and eat a good meal. It was to act as though it had already happened. I believe that as I was going downstairs I was feeling better practically every step of the way. I was acting as though it had already been healed. I think it is important that we act like this. Someone has suggested that it is almost like a game of draughts, that God is longing to make his move, but he won't make his move until you have made yours. You have got to make your move of faith, and then he'll make his move and bring about the healing.

Is healing always immediate?

Not necessarily, I think. I believe there may end up being an exercise of faith for some time, sometimes over a special issue, maybe a real battle for a week or two or longer. I don't fully understand this, but I believe that sometimes when we claim healing there may be a colossal battle. The devil may bring every possible attack, and bring back the symptoms, and we need to counter this. I felt some attacks last night and I had to counter it by saying 'It is written...' and quoted one or two scriptures at him.

I think also that there is a little difference here between a healing and a miracle. I believe that one of the differences is that a healing may be slightly more gradual than a miracle. You get a marvellous miracle like the cripple at the gate called 'Beautiful', who leaps to his feet, rushing around, praising God, shouting praise, leaping around all over the place. But on the other hand you get situations where healing begins at the moment when the Lord says so but it may take a little time. When the nobleman comes to Jesus about his son being ill and Jesus says, *'Go, your son will live'* (John 4:50). The gospel tells us, *'While he was still on the way, his servants met him with the news that his boy was living.'* It was not his son who met him but the servants met him and told him this. *'When he inquired as to the time when his son got better, they said to him, "Yesterday, at one in the afternoon, the fever left him"'* (John 4:51-52). It is interesting that when Jesus said so he began to get better. But he wasn't fit enough to rush to see his father and say, 'look, I'm well now'. I think there is a point there – the boy began to mend but he was still weak, there had just been the beginning of his healing. About two years ago we were privileged to pray with a girl in hospital who was wonderfully healed. She started to heal the day that we prayed for her, in fact the moment we prayed for her. However, it took her a week before she was out of hospital and fully recovered.

What if it doesn't work?

Well, I hope I can answer like this: this is the wrong question to ask. I think that if you are asking this before you step out in faith, then it is not likely to work. Last night, I just knew it was going to work because God's word said so. Whereas a couple of days before I wasn't too sure. I let the word of God give me faith. *'Faith comes from hearing the message, and the message is heard through the word about Christ'* (Romans 10:17). I knew it was going to work; God said so. I would suggest, if you are not sure whether it is going to work or not, it is most important to feed your faith by God's word and to be encouraged by the faith of other Christians too. Again, this man at the gate called 'Beautiful' had the faith to be made well, he was listening to Paul. Paul knew that these things worked. And as he listened to someone who knew that they worked, so his own faith grew.

In this we are not just fighting a lone battle, that I can get rid of all my sicknesses by my faith. That's nonsense. It's not your faith anyway; it's God's who gives it to you. But he may give it to you with the encouragement of other Christians. Then it may be that within the body, God will give gifts of healing to some people. So don't feel that the whole burden of faith is on your shoulders alone; it's not. When you're feeling ill, one of the last things that you want to think is 'it's all due to my faith', or my lack of faith. It is very important not to feel that you are responsible for remaining sick. There may be things that God has got to put right but we are also, the rest of us, responsible for being part of the body of Christ and trying to help the person who is carrying the burden at the moment.

Are doctors and medicines not necessary?

I think if we were able to live at this level of faith all the time, then it would probably be true that we could walk trusting that the Lord would provide us with everything, just like that. And maybe there are some people who do and can live like that. Praise God for them. But most of us are guilty of unbelief an awful lot of the time. I only have to know my own heart to say that. Therefore I believe, of course, that God does use means which may not bring glory to himself in quite the same way as miraculous healing. But of course he uses doctors, medicines and treatments. We can thank God for every single one of these.

But above all, let's take to heart these grounds for healing. I hope I have encouraged you that God has said a great deal about this in his word. We need to pray to have the faith to act and that all of us may have a compassion for others who are in need, that we may in some full measure minister the compassion and healing of Christ to those who are hurting and sick.

CHAPTER THREE

CREATION HEALED

...your kingdom come, your will be done, on earth as it is in heaven. (Matthew 6:10)

What is the Kingdom of God? It's a very important question because the Kingdom of God was the main thrust of the ministry and message of Jesus. We read in Mark 1, for example, just after his baptism,

> *After John was put in prison, Jesus went into Galilee, proclaiming the good news of God. 'The time has come,' he said. 'The kingdom of God has come near. Repent and believe the good news!'* (Mark 1:14)

So, what is the Kingdom of God? The answer is - the reign or rule of God. So that when we pray 'your kingdom come' we are praying that God's rule will extend into the hearts and homes of more and more people, and indeed into the very structures of our society. That everything will come under his control.

Now a couple of introductory points, First, and I think this is the best definition of the Kingdom of God I have ever come across, the Kingdom of God is creation healed. That's actually a definition by Hans Küng, the Roman Catholic theologian. Creation's healing starts with the individual because our lives need to be healed or reconciled to God. Often, churches concentrate most effort on trying to make the prodigal feel

43

more comfortable in his pigsty instead of calling him home to the father. But individuals are naturally far away from God. They are in a far off country, like the prodigal, and we need to call people to be reconciled to God. But it doesn't stop there because an individual, as soon as they belong to Christ, also belongs to the body of Christ, the Church.

As the great South African missiologist David Bosch put it, 'Christianity that does not begin with the individual and his experience with God does not begin at all, but Christianity that ends with the individual, ends.' There's no such thing as just me and my saviour. Certainly, he wants to be the saviour of every one of us, but then we become part of his living body, the Church.

God's ultimate purpose is not just for individual salvation - not just for the church, that we might have a great time. No, taking the words of Paul in Ephesians 1:10, God's ultimate purpose is to unite all things in him, in Christ. Everything in the whole of creation. In other words, everything is to come under the rule of God, or the lordship of Christ. And 'everything' includes the media and education; employment and defence; marriage and the family; sexual relationships; physical and mental health. It includes absolutely everything. Therefore Christians are to be concerned and involved in every aspect of society because every area of life matters to God. God's Kingdom is creation healed.

The second introductory point is that God's Kingdom is both now, and not yet. It is now because Christ has now come, as king and saviour. Therefore we see something of the reality of the Kingdom of God here and now. But it will not yet be completed or consummated until Christ comes again in his power and glory. John expresses it very well in 1 John 3:2 where he says this,

Dear friends, now we are children of God, and what we will be has not yet been made known. But we know that when Christ appears, we shall be like him, for we shall see him as he is.

Therefore we live in what is sometimes called 'the overlap'. Perhaps I can describe it like this: you have the kingdom of this world which has been going now for a long time, but a time will come when it will all stop. This world is coming to an end, and no-one knows that day and hour but it will be when Christ returns in power and glory. When Christ came into this world with it's fallen kingdom for the first time, he brought in a new age, the Kingdom of God, which is going to go on and on and on for all eternity. And therefore between Christ's first coming and his second coming is the overlap of the two kingdoms. And we should see more and more of the reality and power of the Kingdom of God in this world as we live in the Kingdom of God; as we submit to the rule and reign of God; and by faith see the power of God coming into our midst. We won't see it perfectly, we won't see everyone turning to Jesus Christ, we won't see everyone healed. We won't see the whole of creation healed this side of Christ's return. But the more we live in the light and the truth and the power and the reality of the Kingdom of God, we shall see more and more of it happening here on earth.

Let's look at three areas of healing which are all part of the Kingdom of God. There are others, but I'm going to concentrate on these three, and mention the first two fairly briefly and the third in a little more detail.

The healing of our lives

Immediately after Jesus said, *'the kingdom of God has come near. Repent and believe the good news!'* (Mark 1:15), he went along and saw various individuals.

Here was Simon. He said, 'Simon, come and follow me.' And then he saw Andrew, 'Andrew, come and follow me.' 'James, come and follow me.' 'John, come and follow me.' And he called people from what they were doing, to follow him, *'and I will send you out to fish for people.'* (Mark 1:17). He gave a tremendous sense of purpose to their lives, as indeed he does today, when we hear his call and experience the healing of our lives as we are brought into tune with our Father who is in heaven.

One of the homes that Jesus loved to visit was the home of Mary, Martha and Lazarus, two sisters and a brother. They loved him and he loved being with them. They were learning what it was to follow Jesus and to experience this healing in their own lives. The Gospels give a hint that perhaps Mary was a little quicker at learning this than Martha. Jesus was having supper with them and Mary was quietly listening to him, sitting at his feet. Martha was charging around, and Jesus had to say to her very gently,

> *Martha, Martha, you are worried and upset about many things, but few things are needed—or indeed only one. Mary has chosen what is better, and it will not be taken away from her.* (Luke 10:41)

Sometimes our minds can be just charging around, flustering with a thousand and one things, rather like traffic in the middle of a rush hour. What ultimately matters at the end of the day is not all these thousand and one things but actually abiding in the love of Jesus. I think we all have some sympathy with Martha, we all have some understanding of the woman who said 'I always feel bad when I feel good, for fear I am going to feel worse tomorrow.' We know that life is pretty rough and tough and we are anxious about many things, but you know when I was very seriously ill earlier this year, I thought to myself: 'you know the number of times you're uptight and anxious and worried and fretting about things, but when it comes to the crunch the only thing that really matters is your relationship with the Lord and your relationship with other people'.

Life is essentially about relationships and we can get so flustered about all sorts of things. And Jesus says to us, 'Calm down, one thing is needed. Spend time with me and developing a relationship with me. Spend time with other people, developing a relationship with other people.' Of course we have to do 101 things as well, but at the heart of the matter those relationships are vital.

'Now,' said Jesus as he came, bringing about the healing of our lives, 'the Kingdom of God has come near. Repent!' Repent of your unbelief, repent of all the things that cause confusion and mess in your life. Repent for all the tearing around, all these anxious, worried, fearful thoughts. Repent and believe in the gospel, the good news that the Kingdom of God is here, that God is in control, that the government is upon his shoulders. The Lord reigns! Jesus is King!

As we really submit to all that, repent of our foolishness and submit to his lordship, his control, his reign in our lives, surrendering everything to him, then we allow his Holy Spirit to come and fill our lives and enable us to do what we cannot do in our own strength anyway. He longs to help us. If only we repent of trying to work and live without him on the one hand, and open our hearts to him on the other hand.

This illustration is a simple way of explaining what it means for God to come by his Spirit and help us, if we are willing for Jesus to be King of our lives: if I put on my wrist a glove, and hold a book in my hand, and say 'glove, pick up that book,' it can't do it. If I come and show it what to do - 'now, glove, pick up that book' - it still can't do it. God the Father has told us what to do but you and I can't do it. God the Son has come down from heaven and given us a perfect example, but we still can't do it. What the glove needs, and what you and I need, is a living power within. When the power of the Holy Spirit is within us, then we can begin to do what God the Father has told us and what God the Son has shown us.

This has another interesting little point to it. Every true Christian has the Holy Spirit within them, otherwise they would not be a Christian at all. When we give our life to Christ, he gives his life to us by the Spirit. But not every true Christian is filled with the Spirit. Now if I put my hand sort of in the glove, then the glove can do some things, it can push the book around, but it can't work as I want it to work. It's only as the glove yields fully to my hand, and allows the power of my hand to fill every part of the glove, that it can work as I want it to work. And it's only when you and I yield fully to Jesus as King of our lives, submit to the reign and rule of God in our lives, and allow his Spirit to fill every part of our lives, that we can begin to work as God wants us to.

That is what is involved when we pray 'your kingdom come', and that involves the healing of our lives. 'Your will be done.'

The healing of our relationships

During my illness these last months, I've received literally thousands of letters from many parts of the world, many of them incredibly encouraging, just one or two not so encouraging. Various ones told me I was sick with cancer because I had sinned against God in some way or another, urging me to repent of all kinds of things, including being a member of the Anglican Church! I thought that was just a little bit unfair. In fact I received quite a few strange letters and I was tempted to do what a US senator once did when he received odd letters: he photocopied the letter, returned it to the person who had sent it, and added a note saying 'I thought you ought to know that some absolute crackpot has sent me a letter using your name and address'.

Of all the many letters I received, two of the most moving ones came from a former INLA terrorist in Northern Ireland who was part of the 'dirty blanket' protest in the Maze Prison for 3½ years and was on a 55-day hunger strike along with the IRA member Bobby Sands. His name was Liam McCloskey. Liam McCloskey was on hunger strike and right on the threshold of death, but against his will his mother intervened and had him force-fed.

Unlike Bobby Sands, McCloskey lived, although he was very angry about that at the time. Coming to the very threshold of death made him think about his life and that brought him to Jesus Christ. He became a very fine Christian and I am told his witness in prisons is a remarkable one. He wrote me two very long letters, urging me to keep my eyes on Jesus, not to be afraid of death, telling me how much God loved me. I found the letter extremely moving, and he added this: 'it is my hope that we who have been through violent organisations can come together in Jesus to spread the message of love and reconciliation in a hate-filled society. Only God can bring peace and harmony.' Now who in the history of the world can heal relationships like that, apart from Jesus Christ?

That is the kind of healing of relationships that God is doing all over the world. It's tremendously important that we let that healing of relationships filter through to every part of our lives, especially in our churches and fellowships.

Nothing quenches the Holy Spirit as much as bad relationships among Christians. Yet time and time again I find it happening in churches that A and B have a quarrel that is not resolved. So A goes off to C and talks about it and maybe exaggerates what B's been saying and doing. Then B goes off to D and talks about what A has been doing, and exaggerates that a little bit. So now you've got two little groups, then E hears about it and is horrified and goes off to talk to F. So now you've got three little groups. Time and time again I see the beginnings of tensions and splits in churches and fellowships growing, just because we don't allow Christ to be king of our relationships. We don't bring our relationships under the rule or reign of God. That is absolutely vital.

The apostle Paul wrote to the Galatians,

> *If you keep on biting and devouring each other, watch out or you will be destroyed by each other.* (Galatians 5:15)

And sadly that is exactly what sometimes goes on, as God longs to heal our relationships. Therefore when we pray 'your kingdom come', we pray not only for the healing of our personal lives but the healing of our relationships and we cannot begin to see our relationships healed in society, unless first we can demonstrate that we are his disciples by the love we have for one another.

The healing of our diseases

Jesus not only proclaimed the Kingdom of God with his words, he demonstrated it by the many healings and signs and wonders that he constantly did. For example, in Matthew 4:23,

> *Jesus went throughout Ġalilee, teaching in their synagogues, proclaiming the good news of the kingdom, and healing every disease and sickness among the people.*

I know that when I turn to the whole subject of healing, I'm a bit in the hot-seat myself at the moment. I am tremendously grateful to you for all your prayers and can't thank you enough.

The prognosis for me at the beginning of the year was pretty rough. I think you know that the basic story - I had cancer of the colon which had spread to the liver— a cancer which is inoperable. Although the surgeon was a little bit vague to me when I asked him how long I'd got, he told my wife straight out: 'I think he's got just a year left to live.' That was ten months ago.

Every now and again, when we are walking on a bit of a tightrope, it's quite easy to get knocked off your perch and then some things can happen which are difficult to handle. I had a few difficult visits to the hospital the week before last. Basically I am feeling extremely well. I am working hard. I'm doing all the things I should be doing, like sleeping well, eating well and so on. I personally believe that God is in the process of healing me, though there is not yet medical confirmation of that. So if any of you would like to continue saying a little prayer now and again

I'd be eternally grateful. We are not quite out of the woods yet, but I am feeling very well.

Healing is often a puzzle. I remember the first time I anointed somebody with oil. I looked around, couldn't find any oil in the house, so I used '3-in-1 oil' out of the garage. I thought it sounded pretty good, actually, theologically speaking! And having squirted it on them I went about praying for them. So I know that healing can be rather confusing, but I think today there are two major hindrances when it comes to ministry for healing.

The first is a theological objection. There are some who say that healing died out with the apostles. I would only ask anyone who feels that where the evidence for that is in the Scriptures? I can't see it. And indeed where is the evidence for that in the history of the church? It not only happened in the Acts of the Apostles, it happened for a long time afterwards. It happened in small ways perhaps after the first three or four centuries all the way down through the history of the church, and in this century there has been a tremendous resurgence of the healing power of God's Kingdom all over the world, especially in third-world and communist countries where Christians are under pressure. The theological issue I can't accept. I don't believe that God has withdrawn any of those gifts. As we shall see in a moment, they are gifts of his love.

There is also a philosophical objection, which is much tougher to answer because it has infiltrated the thinking of most of us. In the west, we are bound by what is called the western scientific worldview. What we can actually see, touch and measure scientifically, and understand with our rational minds, is not just reality, but has become the total reality. So we cannot conceive how God could do anything our rational minds cannot fully – or at least theoretically - understand, and we are often deeply suspicious of any idea of divine healing.

Now, if God is God he is infinitely greater than the scientific worldview. But it is significant that most of the New Testament healings - which are still happening by the thousands today all over the world - are happening in third-world countries; they are happening in those areas which are not bound by the scientific worldview. We need to be very careful today that we don't miss what God, by his Spirit, is doing and saying to the whole church. We've got an awful lot to learn from those who may be materially extremely poor, but as the New Testament rightly puts it, '...they are rich in faith' (James 2:5). We've got to learn a lot about God's healing power and the Kingdom of God from some of our very, very poor third-world brothers and sisters. Sometimes whenever God begins to work in power, people are afraid. You know, 'fear not' comes in the Bible 366 times—one for every day in the year including leap years! This is because fear is so common.

Undoubtedly today there is a new springtime in the church, and God is doing some wonderful things by his Holy Spirit, pouring out the gifts of the Spirit on many, many people and many, many churches, including the gift of healing. When it comes to evangelism, I don't believe there will be widespread evangelism in our society today until we learn New Testament evangelism - which included power evangelism. The Apostle Paul said he won people to Christ by word and deed, by the power of signs and wonders and by the power of the Holy Spirit. So let's look for a moment at the ministry of Jesus as he proclaimed and demonstrated the Kingdom of God.

Jesus began his ministry after the Spirit had come upon him. In Mark 1 we begin with the baptism of Jesus, and as he came up out of the water, they immediately saw the heavens open, the Spirit descending upon Jesus like a dove, and heard a voice come from heaven: *'You are my Son, whom I love; with you I am well pleased'* (Mark 1:11).

Jesus was then driven by the Spirit into the wilderness—a tremendous, great battle followed as Satan threw everything at him to stop him before his ministry began. When Satan was defeated in that wilderness, Jesus came back and said, *'the time has come...the kingdom of God has come near. Repent and believe the good news!'* (Mark 1:15) To show what it was all about, the rest of Mark chapter 1 shows Jesus casting out evil spirits, and healing sick people. Here were the signs of the Kingdom. But unless you and I are constantly filled with the Holy Spirit, unless our churches our filled with the Holy Spirit, we won't see many healings happening.

Jesus healed all who came to him. He never turned anyone away, he never said 'sorry, I won't heal you, because your illness is there for the good of your soul.' Even to put it like that is almost blasphemy. Remember how in Matthew chapter 8 a leper came and fell before Jesus - *'Lord, if you are willing, you can make me clean'* (Matthew 8:2). How did Jesus reply? Sorry, I won't? Of course not. He said, *'I am willing. Be clean'* (Matthew 8:3). And he was healed. Jesus healed all who came to him, he was never unwilling to heal.

Jesus was sovereign in his healing. There is a mystery about healing, and the mystery may be part of the overlap of kingdoms that we are in at the moment. For example, why, in John 5:1-14, did Jesus go into the pool at Bethesda, filled with a multitude of sick people, and only heal one man? I don't know. If he could heal people with a word at a distance (John 4:43-54), why didn't he heal, in this way, all the sick in Palestine at that time? I don't know. It may be all part of the 'not yet': the Kingdom of God is come, but we won't see it fulfilled this side of heaven. But I do believe that we should see many, many more healed than we do, though we won't see everyone healed.

Incidentally therefore, I don't agree with the teaching which is quite common in certain circles today, that the moment you claim healing, you've got it. It's a fine balance this, but I personally think that the honest thing for me to say—because this is the position I find myself in—that I believe God is in the process of healing me but I am not yet healed. I thank God every day that he is in the process of healing me. But I know logically speaking I may be wrong. I don't think that is being double-minded. I personally believe that is honest because there is not yet medical confirmation supporting healing. But I do everyday thank God that he is in the process of healing me. God only knows.

Jesus healed out of compassion. We see this all through the gospels:

> *When Jesus landed and saw a large crowd, he had compassion on them and healed their sick.*
> (Matthew 14:14)

The key to all healing is love. That love often has to be tangibly demonstrated. I remember when I was in Guys Hospital earlier this year and I'd just heard the news that I'd developed secondary cancers in the liver, it was like a death sentence. I knew that time was short. I've seen the whole gamut of healing ministry, and because a lot of it I don't like, I tend to be naturally a little bit cynical, I must confess. But three friends of mine who are pastors in California do have an outstanding ministry. When I was lying in hospital and feeling pretty depressed, someone told me that these three pastors were flying over to pray for me. They dropped everything and, as I discovered later, they cancelled some very important engagements, flew straight over and spent three days with me in Guys Hospital. That for me was a tremendous turning point because as much as anything else it was a tangible expression of their love, or God's love through them. I could hardly believe that they would bother to do it, but they did. Jesus healed out of compassion.

Jesus healed better in an atmosphere of faith. You remember when the paralysed man was let through the roof on a stretcher? (Mark 2:1-12) When Jesus saw the faith of the men who had brought him, Jesus said, *'Son, your sins are forgiven'*, and there was an argument with the religious people. So he said, *'get up, take your mat and go home'*. And he was healed.

This is one of the great values of worship, because when we really worship God, we are much more aware of who God is, and our faith can rise through worship. I met a man called Mike who was in an advanced stage of multiple sclerosis. He had lost his job, and his hands had atrophied. But at a time of worship in the church – when no-one was touching him or laying hands upon him, no-one was praying for him - he was instantly healed of his multiple sclerosis. And I know Mike still - that was about 4 or 5 years ago - he's an architect doing lovely work again. I've personally met a number of people who have been healed either instantly, or had the beginning of their healing during a time of worship and praise, when faith was present.

Jesus also was hindered by unbelief. In his own hometown of Nazareth, *'he could not do any miracles there'* because of their unbelief (Mark 6:5). He could only heal a few sick people. Jairus' daughter had died, and when Jesus went along to the home, he found all the people weeping and wailing loudly (Mark 5:35-43). And he said, 'why are you wailing like that? Why all this noise? The child is not dead, she's just sleeping.' And they mocked him, they laughed at him. So what did he do? He put them all outside, and took with him his disciples and the parents of the girl and went inside and prayed.

He couldn't pray, he couldn't heal in that atmosphere of unbelief. I know that when these pastors came over and prayed for me in hospital, they sensed in that room, as is often the case when there is serious sickness around, a basic spirit of unbelief, a spirit of fear and a spirit of death. They had to break that atmosphere, that spirit—a real evil spirit of unbelief, a real evil spirit of fear, and an evil spirit of death—before they could command healing in the name of Jesus.

Jesus healed when the Spirit moved in power. There's a rather strange expression—I don't really know all that it means—in Luke 5 verse 17, *'And the power of the Lord was with Jesus to heal the sick.'* In other words, although Jesus was constantly filled with the Spirit, and he healed people wherever he went, yet there were certain times when the power of the Lord was especially present.

Let me give an example. When these three pastors flew over from California to see me, they'd just come straight from Heathrow, and they were simply going to say, 'Hi David, we'll come back tomorrow and pray for you.' But as we were chatting in this little side room off the main hospital ward, they sensed the power of the Spirit falling upon them. And so they started praying. I felt the power of the Spirit of God in my whole abdomen area. I knew God was at work. When someone came visiting later that evening, I said to that person, I feel 500 times better. And he said, 'you don't have to tell us, I can see it from your face'. The pastors were surprised, because they hadn't planned to pray for me at all in that first visit. But the power of God fell upon them. And when they returned the following day, they just came back to encourage. They prayed some more of course, but they largely came back to encourage me. They said their work was done on that first visit.

Jesus was constantly aware of the spiritual battle. Not only was he strongly opposed in his healing ministry, especially by the religious leaders, but healings sometimes could only take place when demons were cast out of people. He met people with a deaf and dumb or an unclean spirit. He had to cast them out before they were healed.

I was invited once to go and conduct a service of exorcism in a major teaching hospital. The doctors and psychiatrists were extremely puzzled by a boy aged about 16, and various attempts to try and release him from his symptoms and problems had failed. They asked me to come to the hospital to conduct a service of exorcism. So in the hospital chapel, with doctors and nurses looking on in case anything odd happened, we conducted a very simple service of deliverance. There were no great manifestations of anything at all, apart from the fact that whatever the symptoms were, they went. The boy and his entire family were converted, and today are a very fine Christian family.

Jesus used many methods in his healing ministry. Sometimes he spoke a word; sometimes he laid hands upon people. Sometimes with a hand he raised them up. Sometimes he put his fingers in their ears and spat on their tongue. Just think of that for a moment! Sometimes he spat on their eyes. Sometimes he spat on the ground, made clay, and anointed them with the clay on the eyes. An awful lot of spitting went on in the New Testament.

Sometimes Jesus had to pray more than once.

> *Jesus took the blind man by the hand and led him outside the village. When he had spit on the man's eyes and put his hands on him, Jesus asked, 'Do you see anything?' He looked up and said, 'I see people; they look like trees walking around.' Once more Jesus put his hands on the man's eyes. Then his eyes were opened, his sight was restored, and he saw everything clearly.* (Mark 8: 23-25)

I remember one rather minor incident when a girl in her 20's came forward for prayer in church and I asked her what was wrong. She said she had blurred and double vision. So I prayed for her and I said to her, 'open your eyes, what do you see?'
She said, 'It's still double vision but it's clearer.'
'Ok, I'll pray again, now what do you see?'
'It's just the same.'
'Ok, I'll pray again, now what do you see?'
'It's single vision and absolutely clear!'
You sometimes have to go on and on and on. I'm a tremendous believer in soaking prayer. Because I believe that God is in the process of healing me of cancer, I value soaking prayer. The team are constantly praying for me, soaking me in prayer in the name of the Lord.

Jesus did not equate sickness and sin. When a man born blind was found, the disciples asked *'who sinned, this man or his* *parents?'* Jesus said, *'Neither this man nor his parents sinned...but this happened so that the works of God might be displayed in him'* (John 9:1-12).

So you cannot make an equation of sickness and sin. Though just sometimes there is a hint of that. When the man at the Pool of Bethesda was healed, Jesus found him later in the temple and said, *'See, you are well again. Stop sinning or something worse may happen to you'* (John 5:14*).* And James tells us we are to *'confess [our] sins to each other and pray for each other so that [we] may be healed'* (James 5:16).

I met a woman who was diagnosed as having chronic schizophrenia. She had been in psychiatric hospital for years and had defied all kinds of treatment. All the counselling sessions went back to a terrible time in her past when as a young girl she had been sexually abused by some Japanese guards in the last World War. That was a huge event in her past and nothing could change that. And here she was, chronically schizophrenic. A pastor, who was very much under the influence of the Holy Spirit, when visiting her said, you are full of self-pity. Self-pity is a form of pride. Unless you repent of your self-pity and pride, you cannot know God's healing. She was furious! 'He was telling me to repent, when I was sexually assaulted at the age of six!' But he made it clear to her that although she was not responsible for that, she was indeed responsible for her present reactions to it all. And she began to repent. Within a year she was completely healed and out of hospital. She is now a missionary, serving God overseas.

There are two more points I would like to make about the healing ministry.

Jesus imparted the healing ministry to others

He told the Twelve to go out and do what he had been doing. He had tremendous compassion for the crowds, for the multitudes who were harassed and helpless. He sent out the Twelve and gave them authority to cast out unclean spirits, to heal every disease and every infirmity, and to preach that the kingdom of heaven is at hand (Luke 9:1-2). He said the same to the Seventy-Two[6] (Luke 10:1-24), and those Twelve and those Seventy-Two were totally inexperienced at the time. But they went out in the name of Jesus. I believe that he gave that command to all his disciples, because at the end of Matthew's gospel where we have the Great Commission, Jesus says,

> *Therefore go and make disciples of all nations, baptizing them in the name of the Father and of the Son and of the Holy Spirit, and teaching them to obey everything I have commanded you.* (Matthew 28:19-20)

It's almost inconceivable that 'everything' did not include some instruction about healing, because it was such a wide part of Jesus' ministry. Certainly that's the way the disciples understood it, because healing happened over and over again in the Acts of the Apostles and the early church.

How is the power and authority to heal released in our churches today?

Firstly, by our relationship with God. Jesus could say, *'...for I always do what pleases him* (John 8:29), and it's only when our relationship with God is good and right that we can expect God

---

[6] Some translations say 'seventy'

to work with power in our midst. Only when we are able in our hearts; our lives; our relationships; and in our churches, to say *'your kingdom come, your will be done,'* will we see his power.

Secondly, by faith in God's word. God healed in the New Testament, and he hasn't changed. He wants to heal today. One church I know well started to teach that God heals today. They taught and taught about healing. But for a whole year nothing happened. The people they prayed for were just as sick. Indeed some of them had got worse, a few even died. And some of those who were praying for them got sick. For a whole year everything happened to discourage them. They were absolutely broken and almost flat on their faces, saying, 'Lord how can we go on praying, saying that you are a God who heals, when we don't see anything happening?' They were crying out to God in utter poverty. 'Lord there's nothing we can do. You've got to do it.' After a year of wrestling and struggling by faith with God's word, healings began to happen. First slowly, a little trickle, and now there are a tremendous number of healings through that church and other churches that are associated with it. I have seen a lot of them at first hand.

Thirdly, power and authority are released by the Holy Spirit. When the Holy Spirit fell upon those first disciples, they were timid, afraid and very uncertain of what they were going to do. But when the Spirit came upon them, thousands were converted to Christ, the lame began to leap, the blind could see, cripples could walk. It all happened when the Spirit came upon them. They prayed, Sovereign Lord, you're in control. You stretch out your hand to heal, we can't do that. But please give us boldness to speak the word. As they did so the place in which they were gathered together was shaken, and they were all filled with the Holy Spirit.

I remember once Dr Martyn Lloyd-Jones[7] asking, 'do you really believe that the room in which the disciples were all gathered together was shaken?' Because the answer to that question will give you some idea of what you really believe about God. Can God shake a building like that? Can God heal the sick? Or is God limited to your own intellectual understanding? What sort of a God do we believe in? Is our God too small? I believe that the greatest need in the church today is to rediscover the greatness and glory of God.

> *Our Father in heaven,*
> *hallowed be your name,*
> *your kingdom come,*
> *your will be done,*
> *on earth as it is in heaven.* (Matthew 6:9-10)

It is as we surrender everything, including our minds and intellects, to God's authority and rule, that we will see his power at work. As we go out in the power of the Holy Spirit and dare to believe that Jesus who healed the sick, who changed people's lives, who healed relationships, is the same Jesus who is alive today, we will see him move by his Spirit. Even though we fumble and stumble, make mistakes and see nothing much happening for month after month, but as we dare to believe in the power of God, so we shall see his kingdom come.

Jesus once said to blind Bartimaeus, in Mark 10:51, *'what do you want me to do for you?'* Funny question really, to a blind man when he is crying out for help. Sometimes Jesus wants us

---

[7] Dr David Martyn Lloyd-Jones (1899-1981), Welsh preacher and influential Evangelical leader

to articulate what we really long for in our heart of hearts. Now the Lord is here. His Spirit is with us. He says to you and to me, what do you want me to do for you? We've all got different needs. We've worshipped the Lord, we've praised him. He's on the throne. His power is not limited. Nothing is impossible with him—or with us who believe.

Let us pray.

Jesus is here with us. I want you to imagine him now, standing right before you, looking at you with tremendous compassion and love, saying to you as I believe he is saying to me at this moment, 'what do you want me to do for you?' You maybe don't really know the Lord, and you may want healing in your life. You need to be brought to Jesus, you need to know his love and forgiveness. The Lord longs to give that to you if you are willing to repent of all that you know is wrong and give your life to him. You may say, Lord I need healing in my marriage or in my family relationships. You may need healing in your church or in your place of work. Or maybe like me you need healing of something physical. Lord I need your help.

Father, you know all the deep cries of our hearts. You know that some of us need the assurance of your forgiveness. Some of us need your love and the spirit of forgiveness in our relationships. Some of us need the power of your Holy Spirit to deliver us from physical afflictions or from depression or from fear.
Lord, we need your help and we believe that you are here. We believe that the promises in your word have never changed, that nothing is too great for your power, nothing is too small for your love. Help each one of us so to surrender our lives, including our minds and everything about us, to your reign and rule. Help us to

receive the full power of your Holy Spirit filling every part of our being. Thank you Lord that you know the cry of our hearts. Thank you that you answer according to your word and in your love. We worship you and praise you in Jesus' name.
Amen.

CHAPTER FOUR

THE HEALTH OF THE KINGDOM

I would like to begin by saying a very big thank you to all who have been praying for me and for us as a family over the past weeks and months. We have been deluged with letters, most of them very helpful and encouraging. One or two slightly less so, some people who find it hard to believe that God heals today, write things like this: 'David, I'm very sorry to hear that you have been ill. Never mind – heaven is a great place!' Other letters I've received are almost like an obituary, spelling out some of the good things I am meant to have done and ending up with 'see you in heaven'. One person actually rang up a bible college to find out how I was. That was about a month after my operation. The person at the bible college said that I had gone home. So we had to correct a rumour after that! Mark Twain once said, having seen his obituary in the paper, 'The report of my death was an exaggeration.'

Just to say a word about my present situation, the operation went very well indeed and the wound has healed. The scan on my liver shows that the cancer actually is growing but in fact I am in very good shape physically. That was a slight puzzlement for me but it does indicate the need for continuing prayer. So if you are able to pray, then the family and I shall be very grateful.

Just in passing, because I know it is a line of teaching which is sometimes pursued, I honestly cannot say that I have been healed. As I have previously mentioned, some teach that as soon as you claim healing or people pray for you, you should say you have been healed. But I cannot really say that without being dishonest. I certainly believe with all my heart that God wants to heal me. I believe that God is in the process of healing me. I believe that I shall be healed. But I am not healed at this moment.

Let's look further at this whole theme. First of all, let's look at the ministry of Jesus. The confidence that we have in healing for all comes from God's longing today to heal people through us. This is because healing and health are part of the privilege of the kingdom of God. You and I belong to the Kingdom of God the moment we belong to Jesus. The Kingdom of God is the rule or reign of God in our lives. Once we belong to God's kingdom, not only should we expect to see healing in ourselves, but also to be able in the name of Jesus to see God's healing amongst us, and through us to others.

When Jesus came into the world, there was a powerful confrontation between him and Satan because in Jesus the Kingdom of God had come to invade the kingdom of Satan. When we were at war with Argentina, it was because their forces had invaded the Falkland Islands even though they belonged to this kingdom. So it is with Jesus attacking the kingdom of Satan and claiming back what rightfully belongs to God.

We see this occurring in many parts of the gospels. In the baptism of Jesus, the Spirit came down upon him, and a voice from heaven said, *'this is my Son, whom I love; with him I am well pleased'* (Matthew 3:17). After that anointing of the Spirit for his ministry, the next thing we find is that Jesus is in the wilderness with a face-to-face confrontation with his enemy, Satan. Having won through those temptations, we see him immediately engaged about his work:

> *Jesus went throughout Galilee, teaching in their synagogues, proclaiming the good news of the kingdom, and healing every disease and sickness among the people. News about him spread all over Syria, and people brought to him all who were ill with various diseases, those suffering severe pain, the demon-possessed, those having seizures, and the paralyzed; and he healed them.* (Matthew 4:23-24)

You see almost the same words in chapter 9,

> *Jesus went through all the towns and villages, teaching in their synagogues, proclaiming the good news of the kingdom and healing every disease and sickness.*
> (Matthew 9:35)

This was the ministry of Jesus: preaching the good news of the kingdom and healing. We see it again in Mark's record of the same time. Just after his baptism Jesus went about saying,

> *'The time has come,' he said. 'The kingdom of God has come near. Repent and believe the good news!*
> (Mark 1:15)

To demonstrate that the kingdom of God had come, we see the rest of chapter 1 being taken up with signs of the kingdom, namely healings. In the synagogue there is the man with an unclean spirit, and he is healed or set free by Jesus (Mark 1:21-28). Simon's mother-in-law, sick with a fever, was healed by Jesus (Mark 1:29-31). That evening at sundown they brought to him all those who were sick or possessed with demons. The whole city was gathered together about the door, and he healed many who were sick with various diseases and cast out demons (Mark 1:32-34).

So you get the proclamation of the kingdom of God and the demonstration that the kingdom of God is now here. No-one could dispute it. Indeed, John the Baptist, languishing in prison and realising that his future was fairly bleak, sent two disciples to Jesus to ask, *'are you the one who was to come, or should we expect someone else?'* (Luke 7:19). Luke records that *'at that very time Jesus cured many who had diseases, sicknesses and evil spirits, and gave sight to many who were blind'* (Luke 7:21). And so Jesus answered the disciples of John,

> *Go back and report to John what you have seen and heard: The blind receive sight, the lame walk, those who have leprosy are cleansed, the deaf hear, the dead are raised, and the good news is proclaimed to the poor. Blessed is anyone who does not stumble on account of me.* (Luke 7:22-23)

Now, that is powerful. The Kingdom of God has come because the King has come! Here is the evidence, and here are the signs. Jesus did not send John a book called *Discipleship* or *My God is Real* (although I hope that these books have some use). When Nicodemus the religious leader came to Jesus by night he said,

> *Rabbi, we know that you are a teacher who has come from God. For no one could perform the signs you are doing if God were not with him.* (John 3:2)

In theory it is possible to teach what Jesus taught, although he taught with astonishing authority. But nobody could do the signs that Jesus was doing, unless God was with him. These were the signs of the kingdom.

You see, the kingdom of God is not talk but power. It is bringing all things under the rule and reign and authority of God. That includes all those areas ravaged by Satan: sin, disease, demonisation.

In this, though the writer of Hebrews makes a very important point about the kingdom of God which we need to remember - in Hebrews 2:8-9 he talks about God putting everything in subjection under Christ's feet. Now, if he put everything in subjection to him, he left nothing *outside* his control. The reality is that we do not see this in the world. We do not see everything in subjection to Christ, yet.

This is, therefore, as I have previously mentioned[8], about the 'now' and the 'not yet' of the kingdom. It has now come because Christ came and Christ is here: the kingdom of God is now with us. But it is not yet complete. It's not yet perfect. It's not yet consummated until Christ comes again with power and glory. What we are to do is to learn to live in the Kingdom of God and not in the kingdom of Satan. We are to learn to live in the age to come and not this present age. In the words of the Ascension Day liturgy, since Christ has 'ascended into the heavens, so we in heart and mind may also ascend and with him continually dwell.'[9]

That is where we are by faith. And we are to live in the reality of that and then to see the power of the kingdom of God brought to bear upon this age to rescue people from sin, from sickness, and from demonic powers. We won't see everyone healed of everything all the time because there is a 'not yet' about the kingdom of God. But we should see what Francis Schaeffer once

---

[8] See page 44

[9] Common Worship: Services and Prayers for the Church of England, © The Archbishops' Council 2000

called 'substantial healing'[10] – not just one or two people healed very occasionally, but most people healed, most of the time.

Healing is a vital part of the Kingdom of God, as it invades the kingdom of Satan. It was so for Jesus; it was so for the disciples, not just the apostles; and it should be so for us.

So what has gone wrong with the church today? Why do so few healings and miracles take place - at least in western churches? I want to give two reasons for this, both linked with one another. Firstly, we have over-intellectualised the Christian gospel. In western culture we have talked it away instead of seeing the demonstration of the Spirit of power. You may know this quite familiar rebuke from someone to the church,

> 'I was hungry and you formed a committee to investigate my hunger.
> I was homeless and you filed a report on my plight.
> I was sick and you held a seminar on the situation of the underprivileged and malnourished.
> I was in prison and you set up a prayer group for prisoners of conscience;
> You've investigated all aspects of my plight, yet I'm still hungry, homeless, sick, and in prison.'

Words, words, words, words. Now don't get me wrong, I'm all for the right kind of words. I'm all for careful bible study and persistent prayer. God's word is living, active and can change people's lives. Indeed, God's word actually brings healing to our flesh and nourishment to our bones (Proverbs 3:8). God's word is powerful, even in the context of healing. But it's not enough to know our bibles; it's not enough to know doctrine. It's not

---

[10] Francis Schaeffer (2001), True Spirituality, Tyndale House Publishers Inc.

enough to study together and pray together and do these things together.

We are both to tell people about Jesus and to heal the sick; to cast out demons, cause the blind to see and the deaf to hear and the lame to walk. We mustn't intellectualise Christianity so much that we reduce it to mere words and propositions. The church today does not need more words. It's stuffed with words! But it does need more power. I don't think that the world around us will begin to believe in Jesus until they see the love of God demonstrated in the power of the Spirit.

The second reason that we don't see more signs and wonders and healings is that we are bound by our western scientific worldview. Now many people don't even realise that they are bound by this way of viewing the world. And for most people, 'reality' means what we can see and touch and measure and understand. It's part of the subtle influence of secular humanism that has filtered right through the church. Now, I'm not attacking rational thought. I'm not advocating for one moment mindless Christianity. We are to use every faculty we possess, including our minds, to glorify God. We are to love the Lord our God with our minds as well as with our hearts and souls. But can our tiny rational minds possibly understand the total reality of God? If God is no bigger than my mind, he's not worth believing in. God is infinitely greater than our finite, human minds. God says,

My thoughts are not your thoughts, neither are your ways my ways. (Isaiah 55:8)

It's almost blasphemy, albeit unconscious blasphemy, if we disbelieve or reject those things that our minds cannot understand. Yet in the west that is exactly what we do with healings, signs and wonders. John Wimber[11] has made this point: that in the 27 best known bible dictionaries and encyclopaedias the proportion given to healing is 0.0008%. This illustrates how difficult it is for western theologians to come to grips with something which is outside their worldview. When we look at the gospels, the proportion is staggeringly high. In other words, in our thinking we are still living in the kingdom of this world and not in the kingdom of God. Now those in the east and in developing countries have no such problems, unless they have been westernised. Therefore, on the whole, healings and signs and wonders take place more frequently in those countries than we see in the west.

To end on a personal note, the scan that I had on Monday shows an increase in cancer. Cancer in the liver simply spells out no hope. It's inoperable. When the news was given that I had cancer in the liver, the doctors, who were extremely kind and thoughtful in what they said, were obviously extremely sorry to have to say so. They explained that there was nothing more they could do. It was rather like receiving a death sentence. Indeed when it first came I fell into the trap and said, how long have I got? But even though I am profoundly grateful for all that medical science and the medical profession can do, I don't believe this is the final word. You see, I've had to realise that the ruler of my life is not a scan but God - the living God. He is the author of life, and he is the sustainer of life. He alone has the keys of death. God is frankly bigger than cancer. I've had to step outside the limits of any secular humanistic worldview to put my trust in the living God who is greater than all, the God who

---

[11] John Wimber (1934-1997), pastor and founding leader of the Vineyard Movement.

heals, the God who longs to bring about and establish his kingdom here on earth and destroy the works of Satan.

What shall we do?

> *Jesus went through all the towns and villages, teaching in their synagogues, proclaiming the good news of the kingdom and healing every disease and sickness. When he saw the crowds, he had compassion on them, because they were harassed and helpless, like sheep without a shepherd.* (Matthew 9:35-36)

They were 'harassed and helpless' not just because many of them were sinners needing forgiveness—I'm sure that was true—but also because many of them were sick, needing healing. If you have cancer or another serious illness, you are harassed and helpless, believe me. But Jesus had compassion on them. Because there were so many of them he said to his disciples, *'The harvest is plentiful but the workers are few'* (Matthew 9:37). Then he called the Twelve. Later he called the Seventy-Two, and then he said to all his disciples to go out in his name. God today wants not just a few outstanding, well-known healers but to use every person to bring something of his power to bear in other people's lives. He wants to use all of us.

Jesus sees among us many who are 'harassed and helpless'. You may need to come to Jesus for the first time and know the forgiveness and love of God. You may be rather dried up spiritually and need to be filled with the Holy Spirit. You may need a relationship healed or to be healed of a deep inner hurt. You may need physical healing. Now the Lord is here. His Spirit is with us.

Let's pray.

Come to God in prayer, with great expectation because the kingdom of God is good news for all who are harassed and helpless. In the name of Jesus, you and I can seek to bring people out of darkness and into light, out of sickness into health, out of all the bondage and ravages of Satan, into the liberty and wholeness of the kingdom of God.

Lord Jesus, we praise you for the good news of your kingdom, not only proclaimed by you but demonstrated by many signs and wonders.

Thank you that you are alive and with us today.

Thank you that you are at work in many parts or the world with the same power and the same signs and wonders that we read about in the New Testament.

Thank you for many wonderful things that you have done in our lives. But Lord you have heard the cry of our hearts, and we look to you in faith that you will work a wonder amongst us. We trust you and we praise you. In your wonderful name.

Amen.

CHAPTER FIVE

THE BEST IS YET TO BE

You may know the words of Samuel Johnson, who said 'hell is paved with good intentions'. In which case, replied a cynic, 'heaven must be paved with bad ones'. Well, there's not much logic in that. But what Samuel Johnson was saying was that good intentions are not enough on their own. Why? Partly because of our own sinful natures - we cannot keep even our own standards of life, let alone God's standards. And also because if we could, then Christ coming to this world to be our saviour and dying on the cross to bear our sin was a waste of time. He needn't have bothered. Good intentions are not enough. We still need the mercy and forgiveness of God made possible through the death of his son Jesus Christ.

I would like to bring you five priorities for anyone who wants to follow Jesus Christ, from the letter of Jude. In the closing passage, Jude gives these five priorities: faith, prayer, love, hope and service. Now Jude was writing to those who were surrounded by an atmosphere of cynicism, scoffing, mocking, and unbelief—exactly as we are today.

So Jude gives us these five priorities:

Firstly, faith.

> *But you, dear friends, by building yourselves up in your most holy faith and praying in the Holy Spirit.* (Jude 1:20)

Why 'your most holy faith'? The answer is that the Christian faith is unique. The 'holy' means that it is different from everything else. For example, who else in the history of the world could actually show us what God is like, apart from Jesus Christ, who said, *'anyone who has seen me has seen the father'* (John 14:9*)*? Who else in the history of the world could actually bring us to God, apart from Jesus Christ, who said, *'I am the way and the truth and the life. No one comes to the Father except through me.'* (John 14:6)? Who else can forgive us all our sin, apart from Jesus Christ? There on the cross he bore our sin, so that we could be forgiven. Who else in the history of the world can actually change our hearts and our lives and can give us a new birth, a new life, in touch with the living God forever, apart from Jesus Christ? Who else in the history of the world can actually give us a glorious hope in the face of death, the only certainty in our future? Apart from Jesus Christ, by his own resurrection, there is none. There is no-one like Jesus.

The Christian faith is a unique faith, it's a most holy faith. Therefore, says Jude to those who are seeking to be Christians in a cynical world, 'build yourselves up in your most holy faith.' For example, if I stood on this stool is it easier for me to pull you up, or for you to pull me down? The answer is obvious. And all around us every day there are forces of materialism, of unbelief, many things which pull us down. Unless our faith is strong enough, we cannot stand firm against those downward forces, and we are unable to pull other people up, into that living faith with Jesus Christ.

So, how do we build ourselves up in faith, this first priority? Well there are so many ways I could mention but I just want to stress two: First, through the bible. Having faced forty days without food and in the most hostile environment, when his own body must have been as week as it could have possibly been, and when he was tempted to make stones into bread, Jesus said, *'People do not live on bread alone, but on every word that comes from the mouth of God'* (Matthew 4:4). God's word is even more important than our necessary food. If we consume as much physical food to sustain our bodies as we consume spiritual food to sustain our faith, I guess most of us would look like those tragic pictures of starving children: weak, helpless, undernourished, and literally starving.

I once asked an admiral's wife if she knew Jesus personally and she said to me, 'we did meet once but we haven't been on speaking terms since.' I think I knew what she meant by that - at one time she had given her life to Jesus Christ, but she hadn't followed it through. She hadn't continued the relationship. She hadn't been reading her bible, she hadn't been praying. Now, how can you maintain any friendship, any relationship unless you spend time with that person? Paul once said to the Ephesian elders,

> *Now I commit you to God and to the word of his grace, which can build you up and give you an inheritance among all those who are sanctified.* (Acts 20:32)

God's word is essential if our faith is going to be strengthened and stimulated. I know that for some people it can be extremely difficult to find time to read the bible. I want to say to those people that God is not a God of law but a God of grace. He loves us just as we are. He understands the difficulties that we are in. He understands how difficult it has been for me in this past year to read my bible. He understands times like that. He understands all the situations we are in, so don't take guilt from this, but I'm saying that the word of God is what you need to build yourself up. It is a vital ingredient and most of us should do something about it. But for those who just at this moment find that almost impossible, then God is a God of love and a God of grace.

The second means of building ourselves up is fellowship. When we meet together, especially in smaller groups, then it's God's intention to give us spiritual gifts to build one another up in love.[12] It's interesting that it is in some countries where Christians don't have bibles, or can't read them, that the church is most alive and active. This is because they have a quality of fellowship with an openness to God and openness to one another. So God is powerfully at work in their midst. The zeal and fire of some Christians who don't have the number of bibles that we have could almost shame us.

A rather dour Scots Presbyterian minister noticed that one of his congregation had been absent from church for some time and went round to visit him one evening. 'Good evening,' he said, 'may I sit down?' And he sat down by the fire and in silence they saw the fire burning brightly. In silence the minister got a pair of tongs, took a red hot coal and put it on the hearth. In silence they watched it get black and cold. In silence he picked up the tongs and put it back in the fire. In silence they watched it get red hot again. 'Good night,' he said, and off he went. This was probably one of his more powerful sermons, and the man was in church the next day! This story illustrates the truth that we do need the warmth of the Spirit of God speaking to us through his word, speaking to us through one another, and speaking to us through worship, praise and prayer. That's all part of building ourselves up in our most holy faith.

The second priority is prayer, and especially 'praying in the Holy Spirit.' Now, why in the Holy Spirit? The answer is because prayer is not easy. It's a constant spiritual battle. Someone once

---

[12] See 1 Corinthians chapter 12 and 14

said, 'our fallen nature is naturally allergic to God and never wants to get too close to him. Thus our fallen nature constantly pulls us away from prayer'. And don't most of us find that true? Don't we find that when we ought to be praying we can think of 101 reasons why not to? 'I'm too tired,' 'I'm too busy,' 'I'm too anxious' and so on. Prayer is like breathing for the Christian. If you stop breathing, then you die physically. And if you stop praying, you die spiritually, slowly but surely. Therefore we desperately need the inward help of the Holy Spirit. Paul says that,

> *...the Spirit helps us in our weakness. We do not know what we ought to pray for, but the Spirit himself intercedes for us through wordless groans.* (Romans 8:26)

We are weak when it comes to prayer, we don't know how to pray as we ought, but the Spirit himself intercedes for us. He gives us that longing to begin to pray. When I come to pray, I am most reluctant—I've got letters to answer, I've got sermons to prepare, I feel tired—therefore frequently I invite the help of the Holy Spirit, who leads us into God's presence, who gives us that longing to meet with God, who helps us in all our weakness. Although there may be special times in the day when we make time to pray—you will never find time, you need to make it—we should learn to share our life with the Lord at any time and in any place. When people today cycle or walk along the streets wearing earphones, what are they actually doing? They are shutting out the world and they are shutting themselves in to whatever they are listening to. Now that's quite a good analogy for prayer. Because even when we are walking down the street or riding a bicycle, we can in our hearts shut ourselves out from the world and shut ourselves in to God. That's exactly what Jesus said in the Sermon on the Mount,

> *...when you pray, go into your room, close the door and pray to your Father, who is unseen. Then your Father, who sees what is done in secret, will reward you.* (Matthew 6:6)

I've actually found it tremendously helpful to listen to praise and worship last thing at night and sometimes in the middle of the night when my mind can go round and I can be worrying about things. I put in the earphones and listen to some worship music. I shut out the world and I shut myself in to God. I find that an incredible blessing. Praying in the Holy Spirit could also include praying in tongues, a special prayer language that God gives to people who really want to worship him and praise him. And that for many of us, and for me personally for many years, has been a tremendous help, especially in times of adversity and sickness.

The third priority in following Christ is love. *'Keep yourselves in God's love'* (Jude 1:21). In this month's newsletter I described something that happened to me on Advent Sunday morning at about 1.00 am when I woke with a bad attack of asthma and I knew I couldn't get back to sleep for some time. So I asked the Lord to speak to me.

I'm not very good at hearing the Lord, to be quite honest. I'm trying to learn, but I find it difficult. But on this occasion he spoke to me very clearly and very powerfully. What he said in effect was this: 'what I long for most of all is a relationship of love with you. And because, after your initial bout of illness you got much better, you became very busy. And your busyness has squeezed out this love relationship I've called you to'. I found it very painful, and I confessed that sin and other things that were on my heart.

I longed, most of all, for a relationship of love with the Lord. That is what matters most of all. It's not what we do. It's not even what we say. But it is who we are in our relationship with God. When we first become Christians we are called to be with Christ. He called the Twelve and the Seventy-Two to be with him and then to go out. And heaven, one day, will simply be the act of being with Christ. So the heart of the Christian faith is being with him, in a relationship of love with him, not just doing this and saying that. Once this love relationship with Christ is the most important thing in our life, we're ready for anything. Nothing can shake us.

There have been some pretty sweeping changes in my own ministry in the last couple of months. I've had to cancel everything this year outside of London and that included major engagements in California, Sweden, Norway, Vancouver, all sorts of places. It has been very difficult to cancel and just stay in London after having travelled for many years. But the Lord has been calling me back to this love relationship with him. Even death itself is not a threat. Remember how Paul said, *'For me, to live is Christ and to die is gain'* (Philippians 1:21). So I'm not quite sure what to do. I'd love to die and go to be with Christ. It's far better. But I think God's got more work for me to do down here so I think I'm going to continue with you a bit longer. That's a marvellous position to be in because whatever happens you can't lose; you've already lost yourself to the Lord. There are no changes then that need be a threat to those who love Jesus, not even changing the style of service or singing new songs in worship. Nothing like that should actually be a threat to us. If you keep yourself in the love of God, you will be ready for anything. Nothing can shake you. It has been said that God brings us into deep waters, not to drown us but to teach us how to swim in the ocean of his love.

The fourth priority is hope.

> ...*wait for the mercy of our Lord Jesus Christ to bring you to eternal life.* (Jude 1:21b)

During the last two weeks I have read a number of articles in the papers on whether or not we are now in the 1984 of George Orwell.[13] For what it is worth, my answer is that we are definitely not, because God is mightily at work all over the world by his Holy Spirit, and he is the one who is preventing society from going absolutely rotten. His revolution of love will overcome all the tyranny and terrorism that the world can ever throw up. Love is the most powerful force in the world. Therefore, however pessimistic some might be about the future, we as Christians should always have this fantastic hope that 'the best is yet to be'. I've used this phrase many times before, along with the statement that 'the hour of suffering is the hour of God'. If the situation seems hopeless; then this is the hour for hoping. When we have reasons for hoping, then we tend rely on those reasons. We should not rely on reasons but on a promise given by God. We must admit that we are lost, surrender ourselves as lost, and praise the Lord who saves us. Life is seldom easy. It may not be easy for you at this precise moment. Paul could say that he considered his *'present sufferings are not worth comparing with the glory that will be revealed in us'* (Romans 8:18).

---

[13] George Orwell's novel Nineteen Eighty-Four was published in 1949, it depicted a future totalitarian society and the concept of Big Brother.

An American pastor recently preached a magnificent sermon. Now I can't imitate the fire and zeal of the preacher, but his theme was built upon the idea of the darkness of Good Friday, with the horrific crucifixion of Christ and the wonderful transformation on Easter Sunday. His sermon went like this,

It's Friday. Jesus is arrested in the garden where He was praying. But Sunday's coming.

It's Friday. The disciples are hiding and Peter's denying that he knows the Lord. But Sunday's coming.

It's Friday. Jesus is standing before the high priest of Israel, silent as a lamb before the slaughter. But Sunday's coming.

It's Friday. Jesus is beaten, mocked, and spit upon. But Sunday's coming.

It's Friday. Those Roman soldiers are flogging our Lord with a leather scourge that has bits of bones and glass and metal, tearing at his flesh. But Sunday's coming.

It's Friday. The Son of man stands firm as they press the crown of thorns down into his brow. But Sunday's coming.

It's Friday. See Him walking to Calvary, the blood dripping from His body. See the cross crashing down on His back as He stumbles beneath the load.

It's Friday; but Sunday's a-coming.[14]

It's Friday, yes, and you're depressed; but Sunday is coming and Jesus is going to lift you from that depression. It's Friday, and the situation seems utterly hopeless; but Sunday is coming and

---

[14] 'It's Friday, But Sunday's coming' is the best known work of Tony Campolo, based on a sermon by his pastor at Mount Carmel Baptist Church. You can hear the sermon at www.tonycampolo.org/mp3/itsfriday.htm

Jesus will give you an abundant hope. It's Friday, and all seems darkness; but Sunday is coming, when Jesus will scatter the darkness from before your path.

It's Friday now, yes, but Sunday is coming! Wait for the mercy of our Lord Jesus Christ, unto eternal life. Sunday is coming when God will show us his victory through our Lord.

The fifth priority in following Christ is service.

We all have different gifts and ministries. They are meant to be different within the body of Christ; we don't all have the same gifts. But they are all there to help other people. Jude mentions, very briefly, the ministry of encouragement: *'be merciful to those who doubt'* (Jude 1:22*)*. The bible says we should encourage one another every day, because of the pull of the world, the flesh and the devil, pulling us down. Therefore we need to be merciful and encourage one another.

How? By a brief word of encouragement; by a quick visit; by a phone call; by a brief note written to somebody. I know there are people who have a most wonderful ministry of encouragement, which is worth its weight in gold. Many also have a ministry of evangelism, as Jude goes on to say, *'...snatch others from the fire and save them'* (Jude 1:23a). And here, 'fire' speaks of the wrath and judgment of God. There is an awesome judgment to come, and we need to help people to escape, to find the love and forgiveness of God before it is too late. Also, the ministry of exhortation, *'...to others show mercy, mixed with fear—hating even the clothing stained by corrupted flesh'* (Jude 1:23b). Difficult words, but it means something like this: we must be willing as brothers and sisters of one another, sometimes to openly confront one another when we see a person fall into sin. We must do so gently and humbly; and yet be willing to speak the truth in love, even when that truth really hurts. Faith, prayer, love, hope and service—five all-important and demanding priorities in following Christ. Jude ends his letter with a wonderful doxology, a thanksgiving to God that he is going to fully play his part so that you and I can also play ours.

> *To him who is able to keep you from falling and to present you before his glorious presence without fault and with great joy—to the only God our Saviour be glory, majesty, power and authority, through Jesus Christ our Lord, before all ages, now and forevermore! Amen.* (Jude 1:24-25)

Let's pray:

Father, we thank you that you love us as we are. We ask that you will help us to pursue these great priorities of building ourselves up on that wonderful faith you have given us in Jesus. Of praying and letting the Holy Spirit help us in all our helplessness in prayer. Of loving you most of all, so we are secure in your love, not afraid or threatened by anything or anyone. Of trusting you that whatever the future may hold for us, the best is yet to be. And by having in our hearts the spirit of service so that whatever gifts you entrust to us we may pursue them to your glory, encouraging, evangelising and helping one another to come to terms with your love and your holiness. Thank you that you are able to keep us from falling, and in you we put our whole trust. For Jesus Christ's sake.
Amen.

CHAPTER SIX

ROCK OF AGES

A prayer:

Father, we thank you with all our heart that you and your son Jesus Christ, by your Spirit, have come to make your home in our hearts. You have come to dwell there. We thank you too that you want us consciously to dwell in that secret place, that wonderful place of your love and protection. We thank you for the promise that you will love us and watch over us and keep us. So, by your Spirit, please speak to us now. Show us some of the riches of Psalm 91, that we may draw close to you as you draw close to us. For Jesus Christ's sake.

Amen.

Why is Psalm 91 so relevant? It's not just for me in my present medical situation, but this psalm tackles one of the most common battles that all of us have to face, that is fear: fear of exams, fear of driving tests, fear of the dark, fear of disease, fear of failure, fear of unemployment, fear of the future, fear of death, all sorts of different fears people have.

I used to be absolutely petrified at the thought of preaching. I remember one of my first sermons, when I was being trained for the ministry. We were sent out to inflict ourselves on one or two long-suffering congregations, and I went to one particular church in Cambridge. The vicar had only just returned that day from a family skiing holiday and was absolutely exhausted. When I got up in the pulpit, with my mouth dry and taking sips of water, it was only about two minutes before he was fast asleep and snoring quite loudly. However, I went on the best I could with the sermon and at the end, so as not to wake the vicar, I just whispered to the congregation, does anyone know what the next hymn is? They told me, and the organist (who obviously wasn't best pleased with the situation) came in with the most crashing chord which woke the vicar up straight away. Now that wasn't a great encouragement for a timid fearful preacher.

This psalm tackles all kinds of fear. The psalmist begins with a personal testimony,

> *Whoever dwells in the shelter of the Most High*
> *will rest in the shadow of the Almighty.*
> *(I will) say of the LORD, 'He is my refuge and my fortress,*
> *my God, in whom I trust.'* (Psalm 91:1-2)

In other words, he's been doing this kind of thing for a long time. He has known many dangers, he has known many problems, and he has learned over the course of time to dwell, to abide in God's presence. So what he goes on to say is of particular value because he has been through it. Someone in a letter I received this week said that an ounce of experience is worth a pound of opinion. The psalmist has already been through the experience of being afraid, of being in danger, and yet he has learned to trust in the Lord. In these two verses, he gives four pictures of security. God is his 'shelter' from the raging storms, his 'shadow' from the scorching heat, his 'refuge' in moments perhaps of sudden danger, and his 'fortress,' something strong, solid, secure and dependable.

You may know the story of the man caught in a violent storm, with rain lashing down. He was in Burrington Combe in the Mendip Hills and walking through the countryside, there was thunder and lightening all around and there seemed to be nowhere to shelter. It was a rather frightening scene. As he stood there, he noticed in a gorge not too far away a little cleft in the rock and managed to squeeze in it and shelter from the storm. As he stood there he thought that this was rather like the shelter that God offers us, not only from the many dangers that we go through from time to time, but ultimately the shelter from God's awesome judgment which comes upon all of us. Some words began to come to him. This man - called Augustus Toplady[15] - saw a playing card by his feet. He picked it up and began to scribble down the words that had come to his mind.

> 'Rock of Ages, cleft for me,
> let me hide myself in thee.'[16]

And the last verse,

> 'While I draw this fleeting breath,
> when mine eyes shall close in death,
> when I soar to worlds unknown,
> see thee on thy judgment throne,
> Rock of Ages, cleft for me,
> let me hide myself in thee.'

---

[15] Augustus Montague Toplady (1740-1778) was an Anglican clergyman and hymn writer.
[16] Rock of Ages written in 1763, it is usually sung to the hymn tune Toplady by Thomas Hastings.

Because Jesus, who took our sins on the cross and rose again for us, he and he alone is the perfect protection, rock, and refuge, even from God's awesome judgment to come. So, from these four little pictures of shelter, shadow, refuge and fortress, the psalmist is saying here is God's protection in every kind of danger.

Though not necessarily from every kind of danger. He won't protect us from the danger. The danger may well be real and we need to live through it. But there is protection in it. It's interesting that in a tremendously triumphant passage in Romans Paul says,

> *Who shall separate us from the love of Christ? Shall trouble or hardship or persecution or famine or nakedness or danger or sword?* (Romans 8:35)

We may have to go through all those things,

> *As it is written: 'for your sake we face death all day long; we are considered as sheep to be slaughtered.'*
> (Romans 8:36)

No, Paul says,

> *'in all these things,* [not from these things but in all these things] *we are more than conquerors through him who loved us.'* (Romans 8:37)

In the first two verses of Psalm 91 the psalmist in his testimony also thinks of four divine names.

God is the 'Most High'. He is the creator of everything that exists, the supreme God, name above all names, which cuts all our problems down to size. If God is such a supreme God, he is infinitely bigger than all our diseases. He is infinitely bigger than the depths of our depression. He is infinitely bigger than satanic attacks of one form or another. He is the Most High God.

Secondly, he is the 'Almighty'. Nothing is too difficult for the Lord. He is the sovereign Lord. And do you remember in Acts chapter 4 when the disciples were threatened not to teach in the name of Jesus, by the very people who had murdered their master? They came back and said, 'Sovereign Lord, you made the heavens and the earth, the sea and everything in them and all those rulers who murdered our master could do was what your hand had predestined to take place. You are in ultimate control. You are the almighty God, the sovereign Lord. Now, Lord, give us boldness. We will go out in your name because you are in control'.

Thirdly, he is the 'Lord', and that really means the living Lord who lives and moves, acts and speaks today as he has always done, as he has done in the bible, Old Testament and New Testament, as he has done throughout the Christian church. He never changes. He is not a philosophy. He is not a name in a book. He is not a religious concept, but gloriously and wonderfully alive. That means that we today can talk to him, listen to him and have a relationship with him, enjoy his presence and know his protection. Unfortunately the vast majority of people today put their trust in alternatives— materialism, money, possessions, whatever it may be—and the psalmist in Psalm 115, just a few psalms further on, contrasts the God of Israel with the gods of many people of his day:

Our God is in heaven;
he does whatever pleases him.
But their idols are silver and gold,
made by human hands.
They have mouths, but cannot speak,
eyes, but cannot see.
They have ears, but cannot hear,
noses, but cannot smell.
They have hands, but cannot feel,
feet, but cannot walk,
nor can they utter a sound with their throats.
Those who make them will be like them,
and so will all who trust in them.
House of Israel, trust in the LORD—
he is their help and shield.
(Psalm 115:3-9)

Fourthly, he is also 'God,' but in particular *my* God. Remember, in Matthew 27:46, even on the cross when Jesus felt utterly alienated from God, as though God had abandoned him and forsaken him - because at that moment Jesus was in fact bearing all our sins so he was in one sense alienated from his own father - he still said, 'My God, my God, why have you forsaken me?'

Therefore the psalmist here, seeing these pictures of security and these great divine names, has three positions of security: dwell, abide, and trust. Stay there, because God is the living God. He is all that I have learned of him over the years and through the dangers. Now when it really comes to the crunch, where is our trust? Where is our security? You may know about a financial crisis in a church where the vicar and church council got together. The vicar prayed, 'O most high God, almighty God, the living God, whose grace is sufficient for all our needs.' He went on pouring out these marvellous words and names of God, marvellous promises. Then he said, 'ladies and gentlemen, would you please sit down.' When they were all sitting, he said, 'the situation is completely hopeless. There's nothing we can do'.

I know a little bit of this in my own experience, because I know that God is all these things - the Most High, Almighty, and Living God - yet when I have a medical check-up or go to the hospital and the doctors say, 'there is nothing we can do,' my faith can be like a pricked balloon. In spite of the fact that I know God is all these things, how easily, when it comes to the crunch, I don't really trust him. But if we dwell, if we make our home in the love of God, we simply cannot lose. Everything may crumble and change around us, but God's love is steadfast, God's love endures forever.

Someone wrote to me recently and he said he had a dream in which he asked Jesus how much he loved him. Jesus in his dream said nothing and stretched out his arms—on the cross—that much. If God loves us that much, Jesus dying on the cross for us, we need to learn to dwell in the secret place. Bishop Handley Moule, when he was Bishop of Durham, had to go and see the relatives of 170 miners who had been tragically killed in a mining accident. He didn't know what to say, so he grabbed a little crocheted bookmark which his mother had made him and held it up. On the reverse side there was just a tangle of threads—no rhyme, no reason, no pattern, no nothing. But on the other side it read 'God is Love.' Often we can feel that the world is like that, and often our personal lives are like that as well: an awful, awful mess. Well through the mess, through the danger, through the pain, God's love never changes.

The psalmist, having personally experienced the love of God in the midst of difficulty, danger, and disease, then has a right to go on and speak to others. In verses 3 to 13 he starts to address other people. I will quickly look at these verses.

Notice the great variety of dangers that we have to face from time to time. Some are subtle: *'he will save you from the fowler's snare'* (Psalm 91:3*)*. And they can be subtle in various ways: by getting involved in emotional or sexual entanglements, drawing a person away from the living God. Or in business, wheeling and dealing with a bit of deceit or dishonesty going on. And that is the snare of the fowler. But the promise is 'he will save you' from that. You may fall into the trap, but he will deliver you from it. Other dangers are less subtle, such as physical danger and disease. *'he will save you...from the deadly pestilence'* (Psalm 91:3). I love the tenderness and strength of the Lord who will save us,

> *He will cover you with his feathers, and under his wings you will find refuge; his faithfulness will be your shield and rampart.* (Psalm 91:4)

Here you have the picture of a hen looking after her chicks - and do you remember how Jesus once wept over Jerusalem , saying,

> *Jerusalem, Jerusalem, you who kill the prophets and stone those sent to you, how often I have longed to gather your children together, as a hen gathers her chicks under her wings, and you were not willing.* (Luke 13:34)

And then there is the strength of our Lord, his faithfulness is a shield and rampart. So he is both tender and strong in his dealings with us.

Then there are sudden fears. *'You will not fear the terror of night'* (Psalm 91:5a). You may know how frightening it is to wake up with crippling pain in the middle of the night. You are bathed in sweat and full of fears. At night time, especially in early morning, things can really get out of proportion. It is difficult to get back to sleep again and hour after hour you are longing for the dawn because of the terror of the night. *'Nor the arrow that flies by day'* (Psalm 91:5b). That could be all sorts of things: sudden bad news or letters which are upsetting.

Well, when the arrow comes by day, we know what quenches the fiery darts of the evil one, and that is the shield of faith: not just the faith of the person who is under attack but the faith of all of us as we join our shields together and make a protection for one another.

Then there is the danger of increasing violence, *'...nor the pestilence that stalks in the darkness, nor the plague that destroys at midday'* (Psalm 91:6). What could be more frightening than senseless destruction in the middle of the day—muggings, terrorism and so on. People are frightened about increasing violence. Notice most of these attacks are sudden, unexpected and unseen. Paul reminds us that

> *...our struggle is not against flesh and blood, but against the rulers, against the authorities, against the powers of this dark world and against the spiritual forces of evil in the heavenly realms.* (Ephesians 6:12)

A lot of people have observed that Christians generally, and perhaps Christian leaders particularly, are under special attacks at the moment, because God is doing a great thing and Satan is all out to stop it. But note that there seems to be a promise of personal protection, *'A thousand may fall at your side, ten* thousand at your right hand, but it will not come near you' (Psalm 91:7). Now this is strange because it is a very strong promise of protection - but let's face it, we do go through great difficulties. There are often, in the bible, truths which have to be held in tension, two sides to the same coin.

You see this in the Romans 8 passage I quoted from earlier. That section begins with a marvellous promise, *'And we know that in all things God works for the good of those who love him, who have been called according to his purpose'* (Romans 8:28). But then Paul goes on to say in Romans 8:35, *'who shall separate us from the love of Christ? Shall trouble or hardship or persecution or famine or nakedness or danger or sword?'*

Hardship is really a word which means that there is no way out. So there is a kind of tension here. Jesus was the son of God who you would have thought would have perfect protection, but he was also, *'...despised and rejected by others, a man of suffering, and familiar with pain'* (Isaiah 53:3). He suffered more than any other human being could ever suffer when he bore our sin.

So what's the solution to this kind of paradox? Firstly, I think nothing happens outside of God's ultimate control. This is clear from the book of Job, where Satan has to get permission from God to test and tempt Job. The cross, when everything seemed to be lost, was the most glorious moment of salvation for the whole world. The second solution is that we as Christians need to have a very clear concept of eternity, and understand that we have only a limited number of days on this earth. The early Christians went through immense suffering because they knew that the best was yet to be. Paul talks to the Corinthians about enormous personal suffering, and says,

Therefore we do not lose heart. Though outwardly we are wasting away, yet inwardly we are being renewed day by day. For our light and momentary troubles are achieving for us an eternal glory that far outweighs them all.
(2 Corinthians 4:16-17)

In heaven there will be no pain, no sickness, no tears, nothing that can spoil our life here and now. All that is good now, will be a million times more wonderful when we stop being a caterpillar crawling about on this earth and emerge as an exquisitely beautiful butterfly living in a different dimension. We need to have that kind of solid hope so that we know that whatever happens, we cannot lose.

Until that time, it seems that there is a miraculous deliverance promised, *'for he will command his angels concerning you to guard you in all your ways; they will lift you up in their hands, so that you will not strike your foot against a stone'* (Psalm 91:11-12).

Now you may remember these two verses were quoted by Satan to Jesus in the wilderness, urging him to cast himself off the pinnacle of the temple because, *'God will command his angels concerning you to guard you carefully'* (Luke 4:10). In other words, the temptation there was to spiritual pride, to begin his ministry in a sensational way which would grab the news, catch hold of people, and show that the messiah had come in this marvellous way, to make everyone gather round him. As I was preparing this sermon, I felt that in some way I had fallen into that kind of trap this autumn. Having felt very well indeed and having testified publicly that I believed God is healing me, I almost fell into the trap of spiritual pride, by taking on far too much work as though to prove that God was healing me. Now there obviously wasn't anything sensational about it, but I think that God allowed Satan to hammer me and to bring me back to my senses. However, if we really are doing God's will, which will be sacrificial and costly, then God's protection is there and the angels will look after us.

Then, in the last three verses of this psalm, God speaks, with six marvellous promises,

> *'Because they love me,' says the LORD, 'I will rescue them; I will protect them, for they acknowledge my name.*
>
> *They will call on me, and I will answer them;*
> *I will be with them in trouble,*
> *I will deliver them and honour them.*
>
> *With long life I will satisfy them*
> *and show them my salvation.'*
> (Psalm 91:14-16)

> 'I will rescue them,
> I will protect them,
> I will answer them,
> I will be with them in trouble,
> I will deliver them and honour them,
> I will satisfy them and show them my salvation.'

So how do we receive these promises and the blessing of God? Firstly, we are to cling to God in love. 'Because they love me,' says the Lord, 'I will rescue them.' This is the great thing I felt God was saying to me a few weeks ago, that he was calling me back to that love relationship with him. Of really loving the Lord with all my heart, putting him absolutely first and staying in that love relationship, holding fast to him.

Secondly, we are to know him intimately. *'I will protect them, for they acknowledge my name.'* This doesn't just mean knowing something about God, it actually means knowing the Lord in an intimate way, as a husband knows his wife. I think in the west we have taken too much of the Greek idea of knowledge and truth, which is knowing in terms of propositions. But the Hebrew biblical concept of knowing and proving is knowing in terms of relationships. We are to know our God. We are to love him and know him in an intimate relationship as in marriage.

Thirdly, if we are going to receive the promises of God, we are to call to him. *'They will call on me, and I will answer them.'* Jesus once said to a blind man, *'What do you want me to do for you?'* (Mark 10:51). The answer was obvious, but Jesus waited until this man called to him, 'Rabbi, I want to see.' And then he received his sight.

Let's pray:

Father God, we thank you that you are the Almighty God, the Most High, the living Lord, our Lord. Thank you for this lovely psalm of protection. But help us in our hearts to cling to you in love, to know you more and more, and to call upon you when in any trouble, that we may know your help, your sustaining power, your strength, and your love. Thank you, Father, in Jesus' name.

Amen

EPILOGUE

A few days after David preached these last two sermons, his medical condition rapidly deteriorated and he died just over a month later. David did not see the physical healing that many people prayed for. However, during his illness he spoke of healing in his relationships with others and in his relationship with God.

> 'Whatever else is happening to me physically, God is working deeply in my life. His challenge to me can be summed up in three words: "Seek my face." I am not now clinging to physical life (though I still believe that God can heal and wants to heal); but I am clinging to the Lord. I am ready to go and to be with Christ for ever.' [17]

Two weeks before he died David was able to say with confidence;

> 'I am completely at peace. There is nothing I want more than to go to heaven; I know how good it is.' [18]

******

---

[17] Quoted in Watson, David, 1984, Fear No Evil: A Personal Struggle with Cancer, Hodder and Stoughton, p171
[18] Quoted in The Belfrey Trust Newsletter of 7 March 1984